# PIONEER WOMEN
## OF THE BUSH AND OUTBACK

Margaret and George Wardle and their three children lived a pioneering family life at Naracoorte, S.A. This informative view of their dwelling reveals many of their personal possessions stored outside the small slab hut. An exterior fireplace is visible as are pens for farm animals.

# PIONEER WOMEN
## OF THE BUSH AND OUTBACK

JENNIFER ISAACS

LIFETIME DISTRIBUTORS
"The Book People"

Distributed by Lifetime Distributors
Unit 6/8 Victoria Avenue, Castle Hill NSW 2154

Published by Lansdowne Publishing Pty Ltd
Level 5, 70 George Street, Sydney NSW 2000, Australia

Managing Director: Jane Curry
Publishing Manager: Deborah Nixon
Production Manager: Sally Stokes

First Published by Lansdowne Press 1990
Reprinted by Lansdowne Publishing Pty Ltd 1993, 1994, 1995

Editor: Deborah Nixon
Designer: Susan Kinealy

Typeset in Australia by Savage Type, Brisbane
Printed in Singapore by Tien Wah Press (Pte) Ltd

National Library of Australia Cataloguing-in-Publication Data:
Isaacs, Jennifer.
Pioneer women of the bush and outback.

Bibliography.
Includes index.
ISBN 1 86302 336 4.

1. Women pioneers - Australia - History. 2. Frontier and
pioneer life - Australia. 3. Women - Australia - History. I. Title

994.0082

JACKET:
Inside a slab house, c.1900. Courtesy of the Trustees of the Museum of
Applied Arts and Sciences. On display in the 'Never Done' exhibition,
Powerhouse Museum, Sydney.
Patchwork quilt cover, c.1943. 200x120cm. Made by Isabel Bellingham, Sydney.

ENDPAPERS:
"Gerity's bark humpy", Palmwoods, Qld. Courtesy John Oxley Library, Brisbane.

# CONTENTS

# FOREWORD

The contribution of women to the development of Australia has been generally recognised although there are many aspects of the story that tend to have been overlooked.

In her book *Pioneer Women of the Bush and Outback*, Jennifer Isaacs provides an unusually comprehensive and detailed account of the conditions with which so many women have been obliged to cope from the beginning of inland settlement to comparatively recent times.

The author has collected information from a wide range of sources including published and unpublished material, oral history recordings and interviews with descendants of early families together with their long-cherished letters and memoirs. The scope of such research should serve as a lasting reminder of the courage, stamina and initiative of those who braved conditions, then unfamiliar to any but the Aboriginals, in an isolated wilderness subject to drought and flood, bushfires, dust storms and invasions of insect life.

Many women, apart from child-rearing and domestic duties, helped their menfolk to build yards, fences and living quarters — the latter constructed for the most part of "wattle and daub" with roofs of slabbed bark. A number of these original homesteads, set up on what seemed to be safely elevated river-banks within easy access to the essential water supply were destroyed by devastating floods which were among the unpredictable hazards of outback life.

Jennifer Isaacs also presents a detailed picture of primitive household utensils and describes the ingenuity with which the women coped — not only making their own soap and tallow candles, but devising palatable recipes combining their home-grown vegetables with bush-grown produce including the meat of kangaroos, wallabies and wild birds.

A major hardship for outback women of those early years was the isolation that not only distanced them from neighbourly company but from sources of supply to which their menfolk were obliged to travel leaving them alone with their children, sometimes for weeks on end.

This situation was gradually eased by the expansion of settlement and the development of bush townships where the outlying residents could gather not only for social occasions such as race meetings and race balls but for the helpful discussion of their mutual problems and requirements.

Such communication led to the establishment of the first outback schools, church centres and bases from which nursing assistance could be called upon in times of need.

The exciting advent of railways encouraged the hitherto restricted coach services to include the home delivery of goods and mail — a task previously undertaken only by the horse and camel teams of "Afghan" enterprise.

By this time a few major problems that confronted our pioneer women had been alleviated at least to some extent, but many were to remain, as part of our national heritage, to comparatively recent years.

The author has included in this story not only the women of Anglo-Saxon and Celtic origin but a number with other cultural backgrounds. Significant among these are women of German families who migrated to South Australia during the 1830s and who contributed so memorably to the industrial development of that state.

We are also reminded of the women who accompanied, or followed, their men from China and Japan in the early days of our goldmining and pearling activities. Some of these returned to their home countries but others remained to rear families of mixed Asian, European and Aboriginal backgrounds. Many readers of this book will have been previously unaware of these women and their Australian-born descendants and also of those women "blackbirded" from outlying islands in the early stages of Queensland's sugar industry.

I am pleased that the author has acknowledged the help and devotion given by so many Aboriginal women to the wives and children of the people who had taken possession of their "dreamtime" country. Concerning this aspect of her comprehensive pioneer story the author writes of the fond interdependence established between white and Aboriginal women that has been maintained, in some areas, to the present day.

Of this and other aspects of Jennifer Isaacs' admirable work I can bear personal testimony and I have no doubt that this book will be of interest to readers of an even wider range than its research has involved.

Mary Durack Miller
PERTH
OCTOBER 1989

Whether setting up the first home or out on cattle or sheep droves women from diverse backgrounds were obliged to learn to make a comfortable camp and to cook in the open. The elegant woman photographed in the 1920s in Western Australia is Madge Jones.

# INTRODUCTION

S o soon after the Australian Bicentenary, and in the wake of the numerous historical works on the people of the bush and outback it may seem presumptuous to offer another account. Yet, of all the published works, none deals exclusively with the lives of ordinary women or reveals their lifestyles in detail, through archival and family photographs and records, as this book does.

The women pioneers in this book are not the "founding families" of large landholdings or even the first in any sense of the concept. They are pioneers more because of a state of mind. In remote areas of Australia these women pioneers, battlers in bonnets if you like, suffered isolation and both physical and emotional hardship. They invariably knew what it was like to cope with little, to make things from scraps, bags, tins and boxes, and to cook a big dinner over an open fire. Most worked beyond the home — either alone or as partners with their husbands. They far outnumbered their more genteel sisters, and could be found as overseers, housekeepers, cooks or domestic workers in the homes of the better-off.

Just as European women were creating "new" lives in the bush, Aboriginal women were seeking or being forcibly placed on another convergent journey — towards and within the new and difficult culture of the invaders — as stock workers, drover's "boys", cooks and housemaids.

There are few older white families of the Northern Territory, outback Queensland and Western Australia who do not have loving recollections of Aboriginal nannies. Yet they are remembered only by a newly-given name, such as "Molly" or "Rose". On the Aboriginal side, memories are harsher — long hours, disdain and inequality.

Other women, including Chinese and Islanders, are included; all were coping with new lives in unchartered personal and cultural territory.

The emphasis in the first part of the book is on the house and home itself, where all women worked hard. The historical documents of women's internal domestic lives are kept mainly in families — as diaries, or kitchen notebooks. The black-covered cookbook, with its recipes for soap, hints for cleaning saucepans or the stove, and cut-out items of interest show women's thoughts clearly, in a way that the more formal Victorian diaries kept by the gentry do not. In the latter the writers seem consciously aware of an audience and the need to keep up appearances. Many such diaries were in fact letters to families in the "Old Country" detailing opportunities and progress.

Photographs which really tell something of women's daily lives are rare. The viewer must find messages about lifestyle in the objects in the picture — overturned washing dishes, flowerpots made from kerosene tins, or the edge of a bag wall evident behind a photographer's lace backdrop. These images, set in context and with oral histories, make a compelling, moving story of ordinary women's lives throughout the country.

The "pioneer" women spoken of within this book lived mainly in the 19th and early 20th century. However, the "state of mind" of women battling in humpies and mining camps continues well into this century. And, as many country towns know well, electricity only reached some areas in the 1960s, the telephone much more recently.

Profiles of 17 individual women are included. These are particular stories or family memories that seemed appropriate to the book and illustrate the diversity of women's experience across the country.

The positioning and pose of the subjects in 19th century photographs reveal much about both the photographer's and society's attitudes to pioneering in the bush and the place of Aborigines. In this photograph, probably taken in Western Australia, c.1860s, the white settlers stand before a productive garden. They could be seen to represent productivity and progress, whereas the Aborigines are seated in a more barren setting, in keeping with the prevailing view that the land, and its indigenous people, needed the newcomers' skill 'to progress'.

The Cook family's slab house at Samford, Qld, c.1920. Priscilla Cook arrived in Australia with her husband in 1893. Between 1893 and 1912 she reared nine children in this hut. The family struggled to survive, growing vegetables and working on neighbouring banana plantations. The brothers enjoyed playing piano accordian and ukelele at family celebrations.

A slab house with well-constructed bark roof, home to an Emu Flat family in 1874. The posed photograph shows many aspects of their life: the table is set, the horse is harnessed ready to transport water, the lambs are feeding, and the young mother nurses her youngest child.

Brush-roofed hessian dwelling at Tarcoola, S.A., photographed between 1903 and 1906. The walls are made of produce bags.

Brush home in northern South Australia, c. 1910.

# THE FIRST HOME

T he immediate tasks for all new settlers, having claimed some land and cleared it, was to build a shelter. Often during the clearing process families lived in tents or tarpaulin structures attached to the drays and wagons that had got them to the site. After this, easily erected bark huts or humpies were set up. In this early phase of settlement it was common for both the wealthy and the poor to use the same materials and building techniques to construct their very first dwellings. If suitable wood was plentiful, slab huts were built. In other areas wattle and daub was a favoured technique and in particular geographical areas local materials were quickly adapted — stone houses in South Australia, built by the German settlers, and timber houses on stilts in Queensland.

## THE ALL BARK HOUSE

Aborigines built houses from bark wherever eucalyptus trees grew with surfaces suitable for stripping. In shape and architecture, many of the earliest dwellings imitate Aboriginal housing styles, although the white settlers lacked the Aborigines' understanding of the environment. Consequently, they were not as effective in allowing for draughts and movements of the sun. Early diarists wrote perfunctorily of the usefulness of the "blacks" in building, particularly with bark. In one such anecdote Alexander Harris tells of a new immigrant who, upon taking some land, found that local Aborigines became quite familiar:

> ". . . ample as it was, the floor was completely covered every day at dinner time by his black guests. Half a dozen 'gins' with their piccaninnies were crouched in the chimney, not only beside, but even behind the fire . . . whilst outside the door the younger men and boys stood or sprawled on the ground talking over their own affairs . . ."[1]

The settlers' overseer, a Mr Beck, who, himself, was "a shocking dirty colour",[2] soon organised the men into labour. He "divided a 7-foot section off from the large hut, and again dividing that into two, with an intermediate passage, lined each of the apartments thus formed with the sound, dry bark of the roof . . . he also re-covered the roof *with new bark cut by the natives*".[3] No mention is made of the expectations of the Aboriginal families involved in this exchange, only that as soon as the dwellings were complete and the settler had arranged for "such articles of furniture as were necessary to render this domestic transition tolerable to the less hardy subject of it"[4] — the women arrived.

The use of Aborigines to make bark houses is again mentioned in 1878 by Mrs J. Foott, who, in her description of her first bush home, in western New South Wales, described having a bark house built "assisted by a black".[5]

Once the first shelter was erected, whether tent, bark or wooden hut, the first furnishings women had were necessarily simply made, utilising all materials available. In many areas Aboriginal women assisted domestically from the outset and in 1878, when Mrs Foott wrote of her bark house furnishings, she also had help with the washing:

> "And now for a word or two as to the interior arrangements of our hut. The furniture was not of a description to require much workmanship; a table roughly made of red gum, and two forms were soon manufactured. Our wagon seats with their cushions made comfortable sofas, and the earth floor was covered with bags, so that the room had quite a respectable appearance. Two logs of gum trees were hollowed out by 'old Neddy' and served the purpose of washing tubs; the clothes I washed with the assistance of a black gin in these primitive vessels, seemed to me as white and clean as any coming out of the royal laundry."[6]

At Mt Magnet, W.A., Emily and William Kent share tea with Jack Johnston (holding baby) and his wife Gertrude in 1897.

An early slab and bark cottage with bark chimney, Orange, N.S.W.

This extended house is made completely of bark. The rudimentary garden contains cabbages and deciduous trees. The lifestyle in such homes was often remarkably comfortable. The window has delicate curtains and the girls pose for the photograph in their white pinafores. "Kal kal", Ariah Park, N.S.W.

Although rough bark chimneys such as this were effective, they were a severe fire hazard.

## SLAB HUTS AND WATTLE AND DAUB

Aboriginal workers also assisted many settlers in building substantial dwellings including houses with split hardwood walls.

Finding a suitable place to settle often meant dangerous trips through unknown territory. Depending on the friendliness of the newcomers, Aborigines were sometimes helpful, although in the journals they remain as shadowy figures still held in suspicion by the writers in spite of their gestures of friendship. They often helped to find suitable landmarks, and then, when a selection was chosen, helped to build the house.

The settlement of a Bundaberg area in Queensland was initially difficult. Climate, terrain and extremely hard timber caused problems. By 1862 the immigration of agricultural settlers to Queensland was at its height and as many as seven ships came to Moreton Bay each week. Many were would-be farmers with wives and families, although both men and women had little experience of manual labour or knowledge of the tropical climate. The late 1860s marked the end of a lengthy drought in this region and like the Hawkesbury area in New South Wales, the stories of ill-chosen homesites where floods washed out selections on grassy plains are legion. Most newcomers lived in tents and few managed to come to terms with the huge hard gums, ironbarks and bloodwoods of the area. The edges of their old country axes were blunted and turned and sometimes, after driving their wedges into a large gum trunk, they were unable to extricate them. Their first huts were, therefore, mostly built of soft small casuarinas and acacias or wattles.

*Above and left*: These houses at Tilba Tilba, N.S.W., show the similar lifestyles of Aborigines and miners in the early 1900s.

# Jessie S. Miller

(nee McClure)
1876–1942

Jessie and William Miller arrived in Australia from England in 1909. They brought with them their three young children, Jessie, Hugh and Sheila, then immediately took up a selection of 400 hectares on the Darling Downs, southern Queensland. At the time the area was infested with prickly pear. They were given the property on the condition that they cleared 40 hectares of the noxious weed each year. It proved an impossible request and they were eventually forced off the land.

In April 1910, Jessie Miller wrote a long and descriptive letter for circulation among her friends and relatives in England. At that time the family was living partly under canvas in the open air and partly in their as yet unfinished log cabin. It gives a warm and descriptive account of family life. Her optimism, hope and goodwill surmount many daily inconveniences.

*Extract from Jessie S. Miller's letter*
*4–15 April 1910*

"I had hoped to be in the house before the cows arrived, but as the first twelve arrive tomorrow week that is not possible. What a time I will have if they all take a notion to wander amongst the tents, or they may

The dining-living room set up under the large tent fly. The family lived in this camp before the log house was completed.

The house of yapunyah logs was still unfinished when this photograph was taken in early 1910.

The living room in the log house. The piano, doll's house and pictures were brought from England by ship via Capetown.

lean up against the house and knock it over. So I torment them, and they do the same to me, and so the time passes merrily. I find plenty to do every day, beds to make, tents to sweep and tidy, plenty of cooking as the appetites are all very healthy. We just get bread twice a week and not in quantity as it goes mouldy so quickly, so I have much damper and scones to make. Butter has to be made too, and a hundred little things such as hunting the white ants. The children have lessons every day and, I hope, are learning something to keep them up until the time comes when they can go to boarding school. They think I am a very hard teacher and keep them too busy. All the same there is much to distract their attention and they often rush off to follow some queer insect or see the strange birds. The birds having deserted a nest close by, they have got a yellow wool chick they made at school sitting in the nest. They have great games and love the bush. They are just away now to pet the wee calf in the paddock. And they sing, and you can imagine nothing sweeter than to hear their young voices as they wander down the plain or in the bush, driving imaginary cattle and riding imaginary horses.

Jessie is a great cook and one day I was in Dulacca she had a great baking, and the day following they erected a shop and we three grown-ups had to be customers. Their stock consisted of tea and bread and butter, over which Jessie presided, cakes, sweets and chrysalis, Sheila's portion, while Hugh sold hen's feathers, chrysalis, drawing and newspapers edited by themselves. What a fine time we had enjoying the fun as much as the youngsters and laughing till we felt quite ill. They

made a whole 7d out of us which they put in their fund to buy me a music-holding piano stool. What times they have with seesaws and toboggans and ships. It really is wonderful the different games children can get out of an old packing case. No more wearisome cry for something to do after strewing the nursery with toys. Jessie and Hugh are great readers and at present are both deep in Oliver Twist, and it is interesting to hear them discuss each chapter together and tell me all they like best.

It is afternoon now and Jessie has made the cake to allow me write. Now it is cooking and she has cleared up all her dishes. Sheila is worrying Hugh to come and have a game, the builders are busy with crosscut saw and mallet fitting log into log, and the mosquitoes are just waking up to worry me. Every evening we light big bonfires, four of them, to try and frighten them away.

All days are much alike just now. Sunday is our quiet day and we have a little service with the children. The nearest church is many miles away, but I believe there is to be one built in Dulacca one day. We have bush ministers who come and see us, one a Presbyterian and one English Church, both very nice. They hold service in Dulacca in the hotel, but as it is held at 8 o'clock in the evening, it is no good to us. We could never get home in the dark.

I must just mention the sunsets and the stars. The first are beautiful beyond words to describe. The blues, greens, pinks, reds, purples, yellows and orange, ever changing and mingling and lighting up the sky all round until one would think there were many suns setting. If only I could make you see and feel it, standing along on the plain surrounded by the lone, lone bush."

19

Wattle and daub cottage at Hill End, N.S.W., a typical 1870 gold rush dwelling. The young women pose in their best dresses for the photograph, one of over 3 000 taken by Merlin and Bayliss for the farsighted Bernhard Otto Holtermann.

Known as "wattle and daub", mud and stick houses were built throughout the country. Branches of acacia or other saplings were made into a frame of sticks set about 1 metre apart. This framework was then daubed with mud to which lime dung straw or animal straw was added. The surface might then be plastered smooth with mud and in some areas white-washed. Other variations of this were to fill the spaces in between with cross branches and mud.

In other areas, bracken fronds and fern fronds would be squashed between the interstices and slurried over.

Hardwood slabs soon shrank, often leaving 5 centimetre gaps between each upright slab, providing an unusual means of viewing the scenery from within. These gaps were sometimes covered inside with newspaper or canvas to form wallpaper. Occasionally the children would be set the task of piling little daubs of mud in the gaps. The mud was often mixed with straw or other organic substances to keep it together.

Before the advent of galvanised iron, all roofing materials had to be found on site. Some foolish early settlers attempted to make a stretch-canvas roof. High winds, falling branches and rain meant that the interior seldom kept dry. In many areas thatching was widely used and in some hot outback areas sod roofs provided excellent insulation. The most common roofing material, however, was sheets of bark. The bark was generally tied on with greenhide thongs as it shrank and could not be nailed. Wherever soft but workable timber was available shingles became popular, although both bark and wooden shingles were highly susceptible to bush fire.

By the second half of the 19th century galvanised roofing had rapidly overtaken all other roofing materials. It was widely used both to improve existing homes or to construct new ones.

A classic photograph of pioneering architecture and family life taken by Richard Daintree in 1869. The well-built slab and shingle house is believed to be in the Bowen area, Queensland. The family keep a pig and chickens, the water barrel stands by the house and an external shelter provides storage and work space.

## STONE HOUSES

In Sydney, the properties of the local sandstone were soon discovered and put to good use, but it took some time for stone houses to appear in other areas. As South Australia's early European history commenced later with free settlers eager to establish their new homes immediately upon arrival, there was a demand for stonemasons from the beginning.

Stonemasons, builders and carpenters were amongst the first tradesmen to settle in the Noarlunga district and were in great demand. The first houses were one or two-room structures built of local stone. They were sometimes rendered, and, occasionally, had thatched roofs, later replaced with shingles or galvanised iron. Miss Ann Liddy was born in 1901. As a child of 12, she lived at Yallunda Flat, near Tumby Bay:

"It was a little stone hut really. My father built it. He meant to build on to it, you see, so the front was a blank wall . . . . This was a funny thing about these — my grandparents . . . built doors dead opposite each other. I don't know why. There was this big kitchen, off that my mother's bedroom. I thought it was the very acme of elegance when they had a board floor put in the bedroom . . . there was one end where there was the fire stove and the cooking was done and the other end was a long table and stools, wooden forms where they ate."[7]

The stone and tin house of Mr Jenkins, known as the "Opal King", 1938–40. The woman is unidentified. Life in such mining and prospecting dwellings mirrors the struggles of selectors and battlers of earlier decades.

Early settlers outside their stone house at Clarendon, S.A., in the 1890s.

## TREE HOUSES

Large hollow gum trees, some of which were burnt out previously by Aborigines, formed occasional shelters. The young German emigrant Caroline Herbig left her parents at 16 years of age and came to live in South Australia. Her first home after marriage to Friedrich Herbig two years later was one such tree — a hollow red gum 20 metres high with a base 6 metres wide. The couple remained there until after their first son was born in 1859, the first of 16 children. The tree is now preserved in Springton, South Australia as a memorial to the woman who had in the words of her descendants:

> "faced death at 17, married at 18, buried 7 of her 16 children, outlived her husband by 40 years. Her life had spanned nine decades, yet she never learnt to write her own name or to speak in the language of her adopted country."[8]

Caroline Herbig's tree "house" at Springton, S.A.

Hollow gum tree logs that were chopped down had multiple uses for a woman desperate for rudimentary comforts. They could be fitted up for babies to sleep in,[9] and were commonly carved to form heavy and uncomfortable seats. An unusual cushioned seat was fashioned by an enterprising pioneer woman in Tasmania:

> "When daylight came I found I had killed a sort of animal peculiar to the country, as all animals are in Van Diemen's Land. It was like a large wild dog or jackal, about the size of a Newfoundland dog, of a brownish colour, and partly striped and spotted. It had a false belly used as a pouch containing the young one. My man skinned it for me and, when we got home, Betsey covered a stump of a gum tree with it; and being elegantly stuffed with dry grass it formed a seat of honour for my wife."[10]

In the Myrtle Bank area of Tasmania hollow trees were used as very early dwellings.

> "As often as not, until a suitable site was cleared and put up as a temporary abode, the selector found shelter and sleeping quarters in a hollow log or tree. Tents were seldom used."[11]

Woman and four children outside "Gerity's humpy", constructed of long sheets of stringy-bark, packing crates and produce bags. Photographed at Palmwoods, Qld, 1907.

# ISOBEL VIOLET PRICE

### (NEE HESKETH)
### 1872–1957

The young, and to judge from the photographs that survive, elegant Isobel Violet Hesketh, married Fred Alfred Price, a telegraph operator, in 1898 in Darwin, where he was the second last operator. After a short stay in Adelaide, the young couple and their children moved to the telegraph station near Alice Springs, where Fred Price was in charge from 1916 to 1924. Towards the end of this period, he bought a property known as Harper's Springs.

At the telegraph station, the children learnt very early how to break in a good milking cow. If the weather was good, for just a few months of the year, they would then have cow's milk. It was an extraordinary childhood for the Price children. Family photographs show them riding cows in the milking yards, shearing, mustering, or bottle-feeding motherless lambs with goat's milk. Other photographs record the breaking of the great drought in 1919. The children, Alf, Mollie, Ron and Pearl, stand delightedly knee-deep in water with their rain hats on their heads. Aboriginal women helped Isobel in many tasks including washing clothes and milking.

Alf, Molly, Ron and Pearl Price standing in the first running water after a long drought, 1919.

Isobel Price in her wedding dress, 1898.

In 1924, while on holidays in Adelaide, Fred Price died. In a remarkable move, Isobel gathered her four children — Mollie 16, Pearl 14, Alf 10, and Ron 8 — and returned to run the property herself. Accompanied by an Aboriginal youth, the family travelled overland for 10 weeks in buggy and dray taking with them three camels, a few goats and horses, and 200 head of sheep. It was an arduous trip from Oodnadatta, averaging only 19 kilometres a day over some of the driest sand dune country in Australia.

Isobel Price with the 200 sheep on the drove from Oodnadatta to Harper's Springs, N.T., in 1924.

A rest day on the drove. Isobel and Molly wash the clothes in holes in the ground lined with canvas.

The Price children on a stack of Mitchell grass from which Isobel made their first house at Woolla Downs.

The children took turns in riding in the dray, on the camels or walking behind the sheep. It was a monumental, historic expedition. Each night Isobel set up camp, cooked and washed. They carried no large tubs so holes were made in the sand and a sheet was spread over the holes to hold the water. The washing was then hung around a bough "fence", near the well.

On arrival at Harper's Springs, Isobel and the children gathered rough Mitchell grass and young bushes to make a brush dwelling over a tent and from this established the beginnings of a prosperous sheep property. Although Harper's Springs proved unsuitable for sheep, adjacent land that they had bought soon became known as Woolla Downs, because here the sheep thrived until the herd numbered 3 000. All meat and milk was provided by 700 goats which were shepherded by the children. As they matured, all the children took a full role in the property management. The girls, Mollie and Pearl, milked, sheared, mustered and went droving overland on horseback.

The completed dwelling, 1927. Left to right: Pearl, Alf, Isobel, Molly and Ron.

Isobel Price with her children at Woolla Downs.

Isobel Price died in Adelaide in 1957. Her daughters recall that throughout her adventurous and determinedly independent life, she maintained her sense of propriety. She was observed late in life walking with the cattle to a fresh-water hole 19 kilometres away — her sidesaddle had broken, yet she refused to ride astride.

Grandson Tom helps an Aboriginal woman station hand to feed the lambs.

Isobel Price with her grandchildren at Harper's Springs.

## DUST, DROUGHT, HEAT AND FLIES

From earliest accounts, one of the hazards of clearing the land, living virtually in the open and doing most of the cooking and washing outdoors, was the dust. In the mid-19th century many handbooks were published in London by those who had visited the colony for a brief time. There were manuals on "How to Emigrate" and, apart from warnings of the perils and pitfalls, they often provided lists of things to take on the voyage, plans and instructions for every type of dwelling and warnings about what to expect. One such account was written by William Kingston in 1850. In an appendix he warns of the first settlers' most frequent complaints — dust and flies:

> "The weather is getting very hot though very changeable. The other day, thermometer 102 degrees in the shade and the next, 56 degrees. The greatest nuisance is the dust, it rises in clouds, which nearly blinds you, and covers everything indoors and out with a coat of very fine sand — so pleasant, especially with bread and butter."[12]

The early warnings of the dire and severe dust storms of the Wimmera and Murray River area were sounded much earlier this century. In an essay written in the time of South Australia's centenary in 1936, Casson wrote of the extraordinary sand storms experienced on the River Murray:

> "Sand is life on the River Murray . . . the blurred horizons and filmed foregrounds which arise from fallow fields, from 'drift' and all the loose country which no heavy growth of any kind has stabilised for years. This sand is with us on every breeze. We spend our lives in getting rid of it — from house, from clothes, from food. But occasionally we get something more spectacular. I recall the last day of 1927 — a year of drought. All morning, a north wind blew like a blast from hell. Before noon one had to work by electric light. The sand, suspended as the wind died, hung over us in an orange coloured pall."[13]

Not only flies but insects of all kinds were greatly feared as they simply did not exist in the old country. William Kingston wrote:

> "This weather has brought an innumerable number of insects of all kinds: flies in swarms, and locusts in shoals and caterpillars *ad infinitum*: but still I like the place."[14]

Some of the early bushfires terrified settlers, particularly women who were left on their own in remote places. Fires would spring up simultaneously in every direction, sweeping everything before them and burning cattle and sheep. In Victoria 6 February 1851 became known as Black Thursday. For six days fires raged from Westernport in the Dandenongs across to the Loddon and the Wimmera. Many horrors were recorded; women and children were consumed with their homesteads, crops and scarcely completed improvements. One settler remarked:

> "With the exception of an occasional spring we reduced the seasons to three — summer, winter and *Hell*, the time when bush fires are raging."[15]

Cleaning up after a Western Australian dust storm, c. 1910. The earth around the house had to be raked and damped down.

Even in well-constructed slab buildings such as this one at Mt Riddock station, intense heat and dust were a normal part of the daily environment of working women. Harts Range, N.T., c. 1940.

The Australian environment veers from one extreme to the other. Floods often follow droughts and for settlements along the main river areas, particularly the Hawkesbury and the Murrumbidgee and Riverina systems, floods were a constantly repeated occurrence very often with loss of life and almost universally with loss of crops, houses and possessions.

Many early settlers learnt the dire consequences of farming floodlands.

Many reminiscences record a grim outcome as few people could swim and many recklessly left shelter and tried to swim to safety. One famous flood occurred in 1864 when the Darling rose rapidly. The creeks were quickly filled and access to and from stations was difficult. Mrs J. Foott recorded in 1878:

> "The sheep were all sent off and the shepherds to the back country and our blacks started with their piccaninnies, dogs, possum rugs, and warlike weapons to the mountains 20 miles off; one active faithful black alone remained. Higher and higher did the water rise, until at last our house was on a very small island, and rapid streams running past it . . . Hour after hour we watched with anxiety the immense expanse of water with foam crested waves, as they rushed past our dwelling."[16]

Remote families who cleared very small areas of land were in the greatest danger from bushfires.

When fires raged some women were needed at home to look after the children to make sure they did not stray, to wet the house thoroughly, wrap the children in sodden blankets and sometimes sit them in the creek. Another life-saving technique was to cover the family with wet blankets in the middle of a freshly ploughed paddock. Other wives and daughters carried provisions to the men, who fought fire in constant heat up to 150 degrees.

In the ensuing mess and devastation caused by flood, fire or dust storms women were required to immediately harness their forces and get to work to restore order, cleanliness and good spirits within the home. This on top of the ordinary rounds of heavy housework and motherly duties could be a great physical and psychological burden.

A family gathers to be photographed, south-eastern Queensland, c. 1910. The children seem used to hard work and the two youngest are barefoot. In such poorer country homes verandahs were more commonly used for storage than for genteel afternoon tea parties.

Many women made the interiors of tent structures surprisingly comfortable with decorative touches. This tent on Mt Garnet station in 1900 is lined with cretonne. Fabric covers the table and corner cabinet and the tea setting and crocheted cosy suggest respectability despite the temporary abode.

The family in this bag and iron home own four wheelbarrows, testament to a great amount of physical labour.

Calico tarpaulins and timber homes were temporary first shelters for many while they cleared land and built a solid home. Queensland, 1880–90.

# JANE O'REILLY

## (NEE McAVINEY)
### 1863–1944

Jane McAviney married Peter O'Reilly in 1883. Their first home was built in the Kanimbla Valley in the Blue Mountains. There were many pioneer dwellings along the Cullenbenbong Creek that fed into the Coxs River. Jane's house, built on a slight ridge with a north-easterly aspect, allowed plenty of sun during the day but kept out the cold westerly winds during the winter. The walls were made of wooden slabs. The roof was thatched and it had a great stone chimney. In this dwelling she reared 11 children.

When Jane gave birth to twin girls, she was many kilometres from a doctor or hospital, but the women in the vicinity were generous in their sup-

The dwelling known as Pat's Hut, built by the O'Reilly brothers who first settled the Lamington area.

Jane O'Reilly's first home at Lamington, a slab hut in which the family lived for 14 years.

port. A midwife delivered the babies and others provided freshly-killed chickens to make soup, homemade bread, eggs, apples, cakes and joints of cooked meat.

When the health of one of the twins deteriorated Peter O'Reilly rode to Lithgow to get a doctor — so fast that he killed a favourite horse in the process — but aid came too late. Jane's 16-year-old son Tom took the ailing child to a nearby spring in a gully and christened her Veronica. Jane planted a rose bush to mark the grave. The other twin was then named Rose; she grew to become a healthy and active woman whose skill with horses was a mainstay in transporting the family's homemade butter.

In 1917 the family moved from the Blue Mountains to the remote and densely rainforested Lamington Plateau in southern Queensland where the elder sons had established a selection some years before. Here Peter, Jane and the children began a pioneering life over again. Although she had been a skilled horsewoman, a recent operation had damaged Jane's balance so severely that she was forced to climb the steep, 11 kilometre route to her new home on foot. She did that walk many times in the years that followed. The last time she did it she was 75 years old and the thermometer was over the century mark.

The O'Reilly house on the plateau, known as Green Mountains, was a two-room humpy with bunks made of poles and chaff bags. The mattresses, made also of chaff bags, were stuffed with fragrant kangaroo grass. The main room contained a generous hearth made of uneven bush stones. From the time the family arrived at the humpy in 1917 until 1925 when they moved to another dwelling, the hearth fire never went out. On this fire Jane cooked for the whole family, frying pans had wooden extensions on the handles to allow her to stand back from the blaze and tea, stews and vegetables were cooked in billy cans suspended over the fire. Puddings, jam roly-polys and joints of meat were cooked in kerosene tins. The daily dampers were cooked in a cast-iron camp oven.

Everything at Green Mountains had to be brought up on horseback. The ducks and the fowls that Jane kept near the house were packed two to a corn bag with holes for their heads to poke out. They were then strapped to the horse and made the trip safely to the plateau.

In the late 1920s Jane ordered a much longed for new stove from Brisbane. The family were proud of their new acquisition but found that it was impossible to transport up the hill on one horse. They decided to dismantle the stove and strap the pieces to two strong packhorses. But once they reached the humpy, they could not reassemble the stove. The sides, which had been clamped together with a large vice at the factory, sprang out of line. There were no tools on the mountain that could get the cast-iron back into position. It was then that one of the sons, Tom, had a brainwave. He found a length of hemp rope and bound it tightly around the stove. He then poured water on the rope and the resultant shrinkage pulled the warped metal into its proper shape.

Guests riding down the Stockyard Creek track, the only access to the mountain until the mid–1930s.

Loading luggage into hessian bags, ready for the packhorses.

Jane O'Reilly.

The O'Reilly women: Anna, Molly, Viola and Rose.

Jane O'Reilly's talents for cooking pies, tarts, cakes and breads were then unleashed and the smells and tastes of her baking are legendary in the family. Six more stoves made the journey up the mountain over the following 20 years as the O'Reillys began accepting paying visitors in the pioneer years of the now well-known O'Reilly's Guest House, which opened in 1926.

Although the kitchen was the centre of homelife and work for most women, interior photographs are extremely rare. This classic portrait is from the Tyrell Collection of plate glass negatives held in the Powerhouse Museum, Sydney.

Fuel stoves such as this example were often kept going day and night. They served the needs of larger homes, stations and inns.

# HOUSEKEEPING

Well-worn collections of notes, cuttings, comments, hints and recipes survive in most families as mementos of the work efforts of past generations of women in the kitchen. These documents, kept and passed mainly from women to women, provide first-hand evidence of internal domestic culture — the archaeology, in a sense, of the home. For most women, the kitchen was the centre of home life and, of necessity, work. The real physical effort required not only in cooking but in maintaining the kitchen area and cleaning all the equipment is often glossed over in colonial histories. Many tasks were no doubt mundane and repetitive yet the individual urge to conquer difficulties or even excel resulted in a trade in hints for cleaning, cooking and coping, that merit more attention.

The fireplace assumed great importance as it was the place where mother was frequently to be found and the focus for all family activity. Bernard O'Reilly gives a warm and nostalgic description of his memories of the central role of the fireplace in pioneering life in the Queensland mountains. At night the fire was banked. On either side of the fire a hob ran along the wall and it was possible for the whole family to sit inside the fireplace on a cold night. Over the fire hung chains, and hooks to support boilers, kettle and camp oven.

Before the introduction of fuel stoves open fireplaces were used and these had to be swept out and cleaned daily unless a heavy log was kept going indefinitely. Because of the open heat of the fire, long-handled saucepans and frying pans were used and variable systems of pulleys, frames and wire hooks helped to lower the pans to the coals. They were known as strongbacks.

Kerosene tins were occasionally used to cook on open fires although they were not long-lasting due to the thin base.

In these early colonial days, as now, women made a range of hand protectors and oven "mitts" to protect their hands when working so close to the heat. Wherever a household could afford it, however, a built-in stove was the answer and following the popularity of the American stove, Australian manufacturers produced designs of their own known as Colonial Ovens. These were basically iron boxes with shelves inside and hinged doors. Others were double walled and set in brickwork under a chimney. These ovens were produced in huge quantities. By the 1860s one firm alone was making 2 000 Colonial Ovens a year and by the 1890s Simpson & Son of South Australia, who claimed to be the first to manufacture ovens of any kind in Australia, had sold over 15 000 of its original design.

All these fuel ovens or stoves required cleaning and blackleading. As well, novice cooks had to develop an understanding and "feel" for the use of the oven — knowing how much fuel to put on the fire and what temperature was required for different cooking purposes.

Experienced cooks could simply judge by holding their hand close to the oven door, but the less experienced devised different tricks. One idea was to sprinkle a small amount of flour on a baking dish and put it inside. Depending on the colour it emerged the cook would judge the heat of the fire. With experience there was no guesswork — unless an unwanted helper put on a little too much wood without the cook's knowledge and then everything would be burnt.

The ritual of providing afternoon tea offered fuel stove cooks a chance to excel. In the time it took to boil the water for the tea, the scone mixture would be made and as the tea was drawing and the mixing bowl washed up, the scones would emerge hot from the oven.

Cast-iron kettle.

Cast-iron saucepan designed to be suspended above the stove or fire.

A cast-iron enamel pot was always kept on the back of the stove. This was the stockpot or the "judge" in which all leftover vegetable water was kept to be used for stock in stews and soups. In some houses the stockpot also included leftover bones, small pieces of meat and suitable vegetable peelings. It was often a gruesome looking brew but one which produced fine meals with a substantial nutritional basis.

The large black "fountain" also kept on the fuel stove was another essential utensil offering hot water at all times from its tap.

Olive Mattick in her kitchen at Gundowda Station, Burrendong, N.S.W., early 1900s. *(See feature on the Mattick family, page 90.)*

## HOUSEHOLD HINTS AND RECIPES

Exchanging remedies, hints and recipes was a country way of life and the integrity of the information was highly respected. In copperplate hand the notes and recipes were recorded in bound ruled books. The customary "copyright" of recipes was observed, each new one being headed "Mrs J. Eams' Soap Recipe", or "Mrs Mary Donohue's Sponge Cake". Sometimes subtle domestic sabotage would be discovered as jealous cooks gave their precious recipes when asked but left out key ingredients.

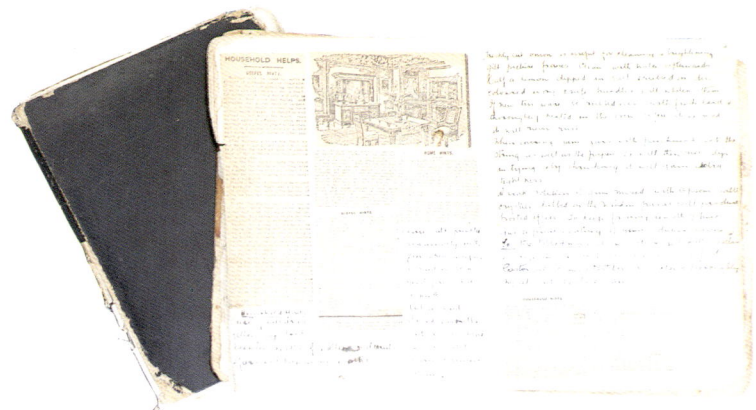

Setting the table at Christmas in the first house in Second Valley, S.A. The photograph is captioned "Auntie Rose in grandmother's kitchen".

Baking day. Biscuit jars were kept full and a batch would be "whipped up" in 10 or 20 minutes. This rare photograph from the family album is of Ethel Maraun, her daughter Irene and an unidentified child, in rural New South Wales.

Handwritten recipe books with cut-out scraps of successful recipes and hints were women's kitchen records.

## CLEANING

Like ships and cyclones it seems that stoves were always female. Both men and women writing of the era of the fuel stove refer to "her".

Mrs Elliott, who grew up on the Yorke Peninsula, South Australia, recalls the pleasures she felt as a girl keeping the kitchen stove gleaming. This was her job and she remembers it fondly:

> "I used to love that. Shine her and shine her. I would stand there all the time brushing and making that shine. And she had red bricks down on the front where if any fire fell out you see, and I'd get another brick and do it. A bucket of water — or some water in the bucket — and I'd wet this one. And I'd rub all these bricks and I'd have them all red — you'd think they were new. I used to love doing that. The stove was the apple of my heart."[1]

The oven required scouring and blackleading. The flue needed cleaning out weekly with soda and water before being polished with blacklead. If little cracks appeared, which emitted smoke or soot, these would be mended with a wet mixture of fine ash and salt.

Saucepans and baking dishes had to be cleaned immediately after use. Washing up was never a pleasant task and, added to this, as water was almost invariably scarce, care had to be taken so as not to waste it.

Homemade soap. Most women preferred to make their own soap. Fat from slaughtered animals was rendered down and mixed with caustic soda. Resin and borax were added and the mass was cut into bars and set in cut down kerosene tins.

Washing trough made from kerosene tins.

Most of the first wave of pioneering settlers had tin utensils that required a good scour, often with homemade sandsoap. Some hints still in circulation in 1911 showed the degree of technical knowledge needed by housewives where few specific cleaning fluids or pastes were available. Aluminium pans were well-washed in soap and water and then thoroughly "rubbed up", sometimes with leather. Most women knew never to add soda to the water or aluminium would turn black. Soda was a widely used additive to cleaning water for other pots particularly iron and brass. The rare, but valuable, copper pots were cleaned with a strange combination of onion peel and sand or sometimes half a lemon dipped into finely sifted cinders. All utensils were "rubbed up" after the cleaning, and, if badly scratched, burnished as well. Iron saucepans have withstood the test of time longest as they were the heaviest and most sturdy. However, they rusted easily, so they had to be cleaned as soon as possible after use.

For cleaning tin, whiting was sometimes mixed with water and ammonia. Bicarbonate of soda, a common recipe additive, was also a basic cleaning aid and if a woman was privileged enough to own some silver it was an excellent polish.

The rough surface of internal walls and roofs of early houses frequently offered welcome homes to spiders, insects, wasps and vermin. Despite all efforts to make the interior more comfortable by covering gaps in the walls with calico or newspaper, it was hard to rid the house of dust, cobwebs and vermin. During mice plagues newspapers and journals published a range of ingenious suggestions for mouse-traps and to judge from the bizarre equipment which remains in regional museums it would seem that it was a preoccupation of early settlers. Large quantities of grain had to be stored, often just in sacks. Consequently, the early bush house was a haven of food to rats and mice, particularly in outhouses or storage barns.

To rid the house of dust, after the laundry was done on Mondays, the washing water was used to wash down the floors and all surfaces. In addition, earthen floors would be swept and damped down. Despite the annoyance of early settlers when termites ate their softwood floors or walls, the ants' gritty mounds made an excellent hard kitchen floor.

Loose rugs, rag rugs or chaff bag mats had to be beaten outside. As finances improved, although labour-saving devices eased the work in the kitchen, the addition of better furniture, crockery and ornaments often meant that the chore of dusting and tidying the rest of the house used up any spare time.

Although household work was often hard, repetitive and dirty, some speak of its rewarding aspects — the satisfaction of problems overcome and surmounted.

Early cleaning, washing and ironing aids kept in the Pioneer Women's Hut at Tumbarumba, N.S.W.

As well, groups of women developed their own hierarchy. Some who perhaps could undertake more, were praised in their districts. The advent of country shows played an immense role in raising the self-image of women as they competed to make the best pickles or grow the largest melons. Such competitions reinforced the self-respect and self-image of women who were good housekeepers, cooks and providers for the family. Even in the much loathed area of ironing there are some who recall this work with pleasure — meticulous souls, who enjoyed ironing delicately worked lace collars and cuffs for special Sundays. Few women have thought to leave behind their memories of cleaning chamber pots or scrubbing the outside water closet!

## CARTING WATER AND WASHING

In the early days, very few settlers had a permanent water supply. Some were lucky if small creeks passed through the property. Others had to rely on neighbours' dams. Carting water was therefore a crucial family task.

Most settlers lived some distance from the creek or river so various transporting devices were organised. Kerosene tins and petrol drums came into their own and large tanks made out of tin were carted in drays down to the river. Regardless of the methods used, water carting was strenuous. If the river was low or the river bank too boggy for wooden wheels to be drawn close to the edge the water had to be carried by hand in buckets in order to fill the tanks.

Some women preferred to go to the creek to do the wash rather than cart the water home.

Jean Frazer and Roy Wheeler carry precious water in a kerosene bucket and watering can, "Inverness", Guyra, N.S.W., 1929.

In the Pekina area of South Australia many permanent springs and streams provided the main water supply for the beginnings of the township. However, some of these dried up in the prolonged drought from 1896 to 1902 and many of the landholders had to sink wells along the Red Gum creek. Wives and young women of the area would congregate on Monday mornings near the creek that ran through the town, light up the copper and do their washing. This was much more convenient than carting the water.

Milking the cow and collecting water, Northcliffe, W.A., 1924.

This evocative photograph captures the strain involved for Mrs Jim Manns to cart water to her house in Wrightville, a satellite town near Cobar, N.S.W., c. 1930.

Handmade watering can in the collection of the Pioneer Women's Hut, Tumbarumba.

Eventually, water was made available throughout most areas of the country through wells, bores and dams as well as the ubiquitous water tank. But if the rains failed, tanks quickly emptied and dams shrivelled.

Wells were therefore a great boon. Sometimes they were sunk 70 metres and many early reminiscences record the relief of a permanent water supply. They were also a danger to the children. A big underground tank or well was often the coolest place to store butter or cream which was lowered down inside billycans or buckets. Sweets and puddings could be cooled there as well, although one humorous anecdote kept in the Pioneer Women's Hut at Tumbarumba recalls how one enthusiastic cook lowered her jelly into the well to set overnight only to find in the morning that a visiting frog had set inside as well.

Filling the boiler from the well for the weekly bath, c. 1900. Photograph by J. P. Campbell from an untitled album held in the Australian National Gallery.

Water was precious; it was needed for so many things around the house: cooking, cleaning, washing, keeping food cool in the Coolgardie safe or in the butter cooler. After the bulk of the washing was done the soapy water would be used to clean inside the house and rinse water always went on the garden. Because of the shortage of water, everyone shared the weekly bath water.

The exciting arrival of a water tank on Andamooka station, S.A.

The McNabb family of "Sunshine Farm", Carwarp, in 1925.   Their newly erected
5 000 gallon tank stood on 16 timber posts.   (*See feature on Clara McNabb, page 102.*)

Four-year-old Jennifer Cain washes her hands by the water tanks. Playing in the shade of the water tanks was cool and comforting in the north-western wheatbelt at Mingenoo, W.A.

Marshalls "Lily-White Washer" was a forerunner of many later machines and was hailed as a marvel in domestic science courses. The photograph is from the *Cyclopedia of New South Wales*, 1907.

The heaviest laundering tasks were made worse by the daily need to wash baby nappies. Until the 1920s linen was always white, invariably showing all marks and stains and requiring the added effort of blueing and starching. Before fixed wash troughs were installed in early houses, wooden or iron tubs had to be lifted and emptied, an arduous and dangerous task for pregnant women. Burning and scalding accidents often occurred.

Wash tubs could be made from kerosene tins or the judicious hollowing out of large gum logs. Most women stirred the clothes in a tub over the fire. It was heavy work — apart from carrying the water, wood also had to be chopped and before the advent of wringers, clothes were wrung by hand.

Early handmade wire soap holder from the collection of the Pioneer Women's Hut, Tumbarumba, N.S.W.

The girls bring in the dry clothes on the Sampson property, Upper Caboolture, Qld, c. 1925.

Washboards were ribbed sheets of glass, metal or wood set into a frame, on which soapy clothes were scrubbed vigorously.

Washing was therefore an intensely physical activity. It required a variety of manual implements now known only through historic collections. For some they evoke the nostalgia of childhood memories yet the women who were forced to use them constantly might have thought differently. Many of these utensils have not survived the passage of time since they were thought to be so mundane. Copper sticks, for example, were seldom kept. Similarly, washboards, wash dollies and possers are rare. Washboards were simple ribbed boards of wood or glass on which soapy clothes were scrubbed vigorously. The wash dolly was an early device which had to be lifted up and down in a tub or barrel to pound and rotate the clothes. Other implements like the posser, a vacuum cone attached to a stick, were worked up and down on the clothes in a tub of soapy water in an action which imitated the subsequent development of washing machines.

Mangles wrung out excess water but required strength and care. Buttons, or even worse, fingers, could be crushed.

The laundry was an outside area set aside for boiling tubs of washing. It was often in the open, but sometimes enclosed in a separate "wash-house", in which a permanent copper would be "set-in". This was a large bricked-in metal container with a fire box beneath, often attached to an exterior tank for ease of water supply. Porta gas and chip coppers replaced these built-in varieties. Before filling the copper with water, grated soap would be added and then the clothes, which were then boiled and stirred with a stick for a good half hour.

Kathleen Blackwood recalled life with her mother at The Rock, near Wagga Wagga, in 1917 when she was 12:

> "To wash the clothes there was tub on a box in the yard as close as you could light a fire. The clothes were boiled in kerosene tins, scrubbed on a scrubbing board, lifted out with a stick. It took all day for a family wash. Then the clothes were put into another tub to be blued. Homemade starch was made of cornflour (Mum would eat Silver Star Starch so we never used it as Dad didn't know if it was good for her). We had a wire clothes line and ironed the clothes with flat irons. Most people didn't have cupboards and the clothes were just hung on nails."[2]

On a Monday morning it was a matter of pride to many women in the country areas that their washing be seen hanging on the line first.

> "One lady, who at times had visitors on Sunday afternoon and could not find time to do her washing ready for the Monday morning display, would make sure her sheets were first on the line by taking the dry ones out of her drawers and hanging them out on the line."[3]

Early manual washing machine.

Even in flood times, the washing had to be done. Mannum, S.A., 1956.

A family outside their timber house on the Andamooka opal fields, 1956. Many elements of pioneering life continue — a wringer washing machine (possibly petrol-powered) has replaced a bucket on the fire.

Washing followed a definite ritual. Sheets were soaked in the copper overnight and boiled next day. They were then lifted out with the copper stick and put through the wringer into the "blue" — Reckitts blue bags were placed in the rinse water to counteract the yellowing effect of the soap on whites. All clothes were then wound through the wringer into the blue. After this they would be put back through the wringer and then out onto a long line held up with a prop. All white cottons, towels and tea towels were boiled and the rest were done by hand. The washboard was used for stubborn dirt, particularly work shirts and trousers.

Washing and ironing for a family of even three or four children was extremely arduous and many women sought assistance from Aboriginal women or others who were paid a small amount to help. The routine varied very little into the 20th century despite the advent of washing machines and wringers as many remote farms did not have electricity or a made road until the 1960s.

The wash tub frequently doubled as the family bath.

"Well, we had a big tub. We had a great big tub you see. One of the older ones could get into it with one of the little ones. They would paddle and splash about having a great time. We got the water from the well, a couple of buckets. Mum'd heated it out in the yard, you know, to warm it so it wouldn't be chilly and that's how we used to have a bath. We used to enjoy them too . . . then we'd start running around, you see, to sort of get dry. But when it got cold we used to have to go inside, put the tub in front of the fire and get in there."[4]

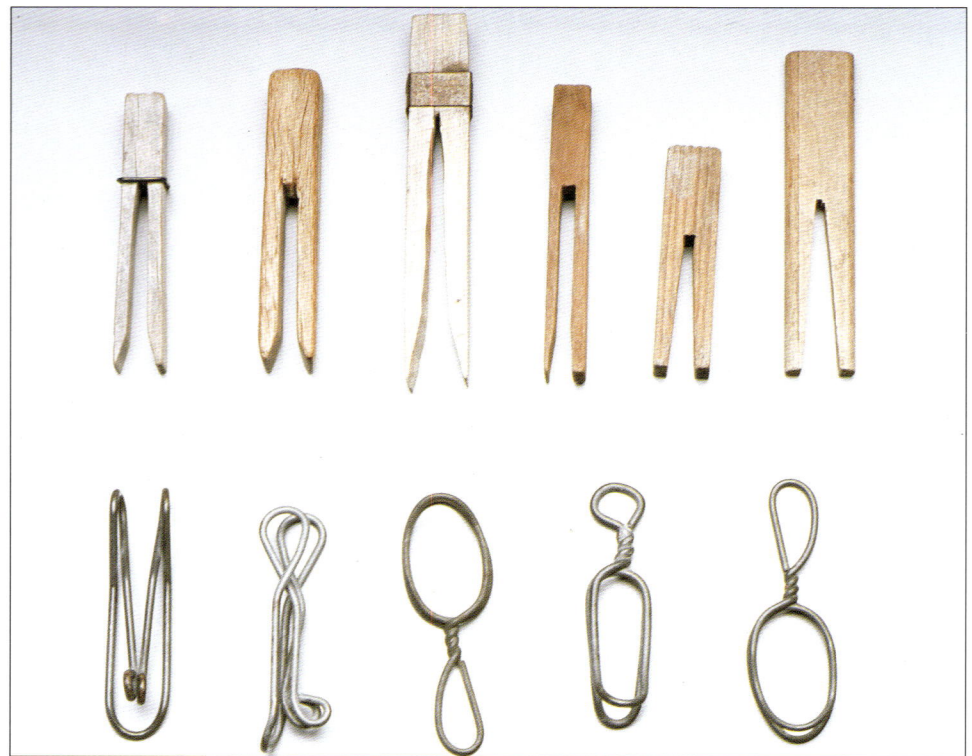

A range of early pegs made from wood and wire kept in the Powerhouse Museum, Sydney.

The camp wash at Julia Creek, Cloncurry, Qld, c. 1921. The woman tends the delicate whites while her male friend washes the dog.

Trough made from a kerosene tin.

# FLORENCE BILTON

## (NEE WILSON)
## 1860–1941

As a young schoolteacher, Florence Wilson lived with her mother in the country schoolhouse at Kialla West, Victoria. Louie Lesing, a young Chinese orphan girl, in the service of a neighbour, would often run across the paddocks to the Wilsons', after being whipped and beaten by her employers. Eventually, Mrs Wilson would not let her return and an "Application" was granted for Louie to remain with the Wilsons. She became a devoted friend and maid, staying with the family until her death in 1938, aged 75.

While teaching at Kialla West, Florence met David Bilton, a teacher. They married in 1886, and later, with her mother and Louie, moved to the school at Leviathan Reef, 8 kilometres from the goldmining town of Maryborough, Victoria. There,

Florence would walk across the paddocks to meet another teacher, with whom she travelled by horse and buggy to the school at Timor West, where she was an assistant teacher. After her fourth child was born, she continued teaching, until the Education Department introduced the regulation that married women must retire.

In 1885 David Bilton was transferred to Adelaide Head School, near Maryborough, and the family went to live at Hatfield Farm. With the help of Louie, Florence did all the cooking, washing and ironing, and gardening, growing vegetables and fruit to help feed the family of seven children.

Water was caught in a tank and an underground well, groceries bought in bulk and stored in mouse-proof containers, and meat, both lamb and beef,

Washing day at "Hatfield", Craigie, Vic., early 1900s. Florence Bilton is on the far right, and her maid, Louie Lesing is far left.

came from the farm. Florence and Louie made all the jams, sauces, chutneys and pickles. The older children milked the cows before and after school. The milk was placed in large flat dishes in the dairy, where the cream was skimmed off the top to make butter. The butter was washed several times until all the buttermilk was extracted, then put on a scalded board, kneaded, salted and patted into pounds. Florence would make scones with the buttermilk, and the calves were then fed the skim milk.

Louie Lesing, the Chinese maid who came to Florence Bilton as a young state ward and remained all her life.

Florence Bilton in 1918.

"Hatfield" at Craigie, Vic.

The ironing ritual. A scene from rural life in the town of Drouin, Vic., 1940s.

## IRONING

Ironing was a laborious chore, but something which had to be done, for appearances were important. On weekends and Sundays, most women were anxious that the family was well turned out in their very best clothes and that, despite poverty, they were clean and fresh. Many women remember the box iron:

> "You know, the one with coals in it. It was a lovely old iron — had a rooster on the top . . . We used to get the coals out. Oh, we had two lots of irons because there were others — Mrs Potts, I think they were. You had to squeeze the top and put the handle on them. There were three in the set and they always had to stay on top of the oven. You'd have to rub them a little bit before you started to iron because there would always be a little bit of smoke coming through from the wood fire."[5]

Numerous old irons remain as relics of the endless arduous hours women spent removing creases from wrung or mangled clothes. The most common were the flat irons which were heated on the stove or in the fire itself. When ironing many wore some kind of hand mitt as some irons were dangerous and burns and scalds were common. The base of the iron had to be wiped clean and rubbed with beeswax as smuts could easily ruin a clean wash. Box irons had funnels in which red hot coals were placed. If they began to get cool the woman would swing it around in a breeze to ignite the coals again. Petrol pressure irons worked on the same principle as gas irons but were highly dangerous and not infrequently exploded, with tragic results. Other irons included billet irons in which a block of iron was heated then slipped inside the main frame, and spirit irons which were heated by burning rags soaked in methylated spirits inside a cavity.

Many old irons remain as reminders of the arduous hours women spent removing creases from clothes. The flat iron and the "Mrs Potts" are most common.

## CANDLES AND KEROSENE LAMPS

"Slush" lamps were probably the first means of light that were used in early homes, but these were followed quickly by candles. Few families bought these as there was sufficient fat from slaughtered animals that could be kept and used. The simplest candles were made from clarified fat or tallow sometimes mixed with beeswax. Others were made from lard mixed with alum. When the supply of candles in the household dwindled the moulds would be set out, the fat melted and the cotton wicks dipped in a mixture of water, lime and saltpetre. When the fat was poured into the moulds the wicks were held clear by pushing a stick through them and resting this on top of the mould. After the tallow had set hard — up to a day later — the candles would be released from the mould and ready for use. In the very earliest years of settlement up to the 1840s matches were not available and cumbersome wax or sulphur sticks were the only means of fire making — hence the added importance of keeping embers constantly alight in the open fire. Later, tapers made of wax and fire lighters soaked in kerosene were also used.

Elegant kerosene lamps such as this lit many country living rooms.

Candles were soon followed by kerosene lamps. Kerosene was discovered in 1850 and from this time imported lamps became available in a wide range of models. Later versions used an incandescent mantle instead of a wick, but the glass covers were always a recurring expense as they were easily broken. A task for the children was often to clean these kerosene glasses by boiling them in water and rubbing them with salt when dry.

Whether candles or kerosene lamps were used there was always an element of danger. The lavatories in all early settlements were away from the house "out the back" and there are more than a few stories of young children in long white nightgowns who came to grief carrying kerosene lamps late at night. The woman of the house had to prepare for all contingencies so kerosene lamps had to be full, have their wicks trimmed and ready for any emergency in the night and be within easy reach so that they would not be knocked over.

## PRACTICALITIES, CLOTHING AND DECORATION

Women's influence on the home extended to the comforts within. When the home was completed and the women arrived, bare windows were soon covered with calico curtains, wallpaper went up (even if it was newspaper), and items of clothing were made for the family.

In the early days there is no doubt that lack of materials was a severe problem and recycling was essential to equip a house and farm. Nothing was thrown out — fencing wire had innumerable uses, but for women, the most significant domestic materials were kerosene tins and produce bags.

Mrs Donoghue, a housekeeper employed by James Connell in western New South Wales. The kitchen and living quarters were a tent, with earth floor. The clearly visible array of pots, teapots and other equipment makes this photograph rare and significant.

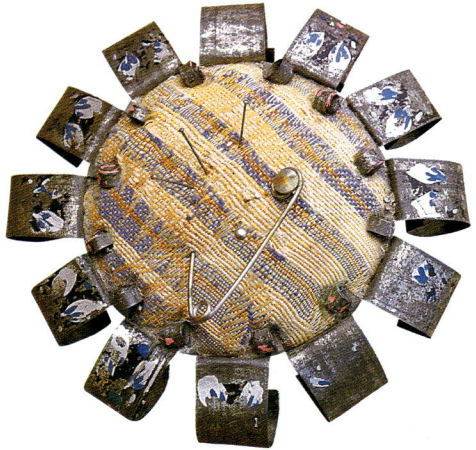

Recycling materials was a complete way of life. Pin cushions like this were made from tin cans by swaggies and then bartered or sold to women at remote stations.

Morning tea. Traditionally, many women brought tea and cake to the men who were busy filling bags or harvesting. These sacks were used in innumerable ways around the house and property.

## PRODUCE BAGS

Produce bags were a great aid to outback women. Stores were often packed in sacks, slung on camels or stacked on drays. Many photographs record the central role of these simple, mundane items — packing the chaff and stacking the bags ready for transport or unloading the dray's bags with three months supply of flour, sugar, and grain. In the background of the photographs are glimpses of the fate of the bags after they were emptied — fabric walls, makeshift curtains, meat safes or even clothing. They were indispensable.

Few early homes had proper beds. In a great many the first resting places were made using stake-supported poles covered by two or three wheat bags.

> "Life in that old humpy was something that would be hard to parallel now. There were two rooms, one for sleeping and keeping clothes — the other was a cooking, eating and living room, which also had a couple of bunks. These bunks were made by putting two poles lengthways through chaff bags, and were supported at each end by two short cross legs wired x fashion; mattresses were two chaff bags sewn together and stuffed with soft pungent kangaroo grass."[6]

All the supplies of the early settlers came in some form of produce bag — wheat, flour, sugar, oats or bran. Each bag differed in quality and texture as well as weave. The qualities of jute, hessian and calico could be utilised by women of the bush and outback in many different ways.

66

A description of the types and uses of produce bags kept by a small shop-keeper in the 1930s gives an insight into their importance in early homes. The store at Holbrook, New South Wales[7] kept sugar of various grades. Fine white sugar was packed in 70 pound jute bags. The shopkeeper would tip this in a bin then weigh it into smaller bags. From this fine, tightly woven jute fabric women made aprons, towels, peg bags and pot-holders — useful in the kitchen and the laundry, but also items which were seen quite often by visitors or friends and which had to look, or at least simulate, a better quality material.

Brown sugar also came in 70 pound jute bags. Flour came in 25 pound and 50 pound calico bags, printed with the name of the miller. If a very large supply of flour was required, outback stations would order 150 pound jute bags which were heavy and finely woven. Fifty pound bags made excellent pillow slips. Twenty-five pound bags were used when hanging salted meat in the kitchen.

The finest bags of all were made into children's clothing — trousers for boys and dresses for girls. These are well remembered by Aboriginal people who grew up in missions or in humpies. In itinerant communities underclothing was often made of the finest calico flour bags.

Fine flour bags were re-used for clothing.

A Chinese humpy near Darwin, 1911. The walls are made of rough woven straw used for wrapping bales. Kerosene tins are also evident.

Chaff bags were hessian, with a much more open weave than the jute bags. This rough material was mostly used as inner lining on walls. The bags were simply stretched and fastened across the slabs to create a feeling of an interior wall. Sometimes they would be white-washed or covered with paper. Such open weave chaff bags were also used for the sides of Coolgardie safes, but they could not be used to hang meat in as flies would blow through a chaff bag.

Wheat, bran, pollard and oats also came in jute bags. Rough mattresses could be made in the shed for workers as a temporary measure by connecting four or five sacks, sewing them together with twine, and stuffing them with straw. Ti e rough sacks could, in fact, be used for any purpose. They could be strung on a frame to screen piles of dead rabbits or used on earthen floors in settlers' cottages. In the latter case the empty sacks were spread on the bare soil or ant bed then saturated and after a lengthy period the floor would be firm and solid.

The traditional "wagga rugs", or "waggas", were used by itinerant bush workers in many parts of Australia from the late 19th century. They were made from heavy jute bags, 150 pound flour bags or wheat sacks, sewn together with a bag needle and twine.

Women were ingenious at making domestic rugs or cloths from bags and whatever else was on hand, including old used clothing. Ellen Bradley of Rosewood recalls:

> "I made one from the sugar bags when the boys were little and things got hard. I sewed old woollen socks and pieces together like a patchwork and put the sugar bag on the back and an old sheet or something on top."[8]

The locals in Wagga recall that in the early 1930s the Wagga Flour Mill would leave a pile of torn, broken or mice-nibbled bags out the back. The "baggies" or "swaggies" would collect these and make them into useful items, particularly waggas.

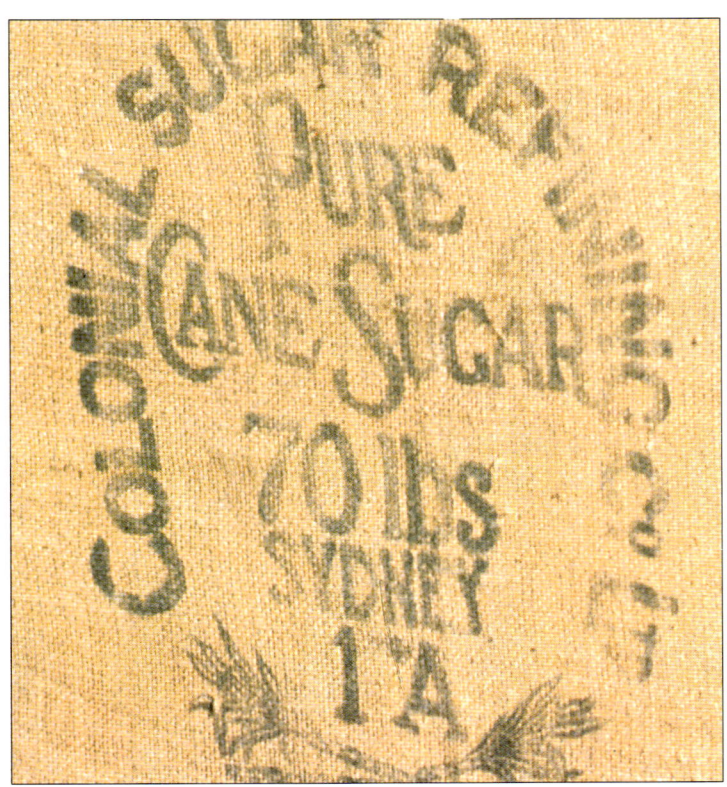

Produce bags had many uses outdoors as well as in the house. Several would be sewn together with twine and used to protect the hands when stacking wood. In the high country where cattle or horses had to be kept warm they would be made into horse blankets.

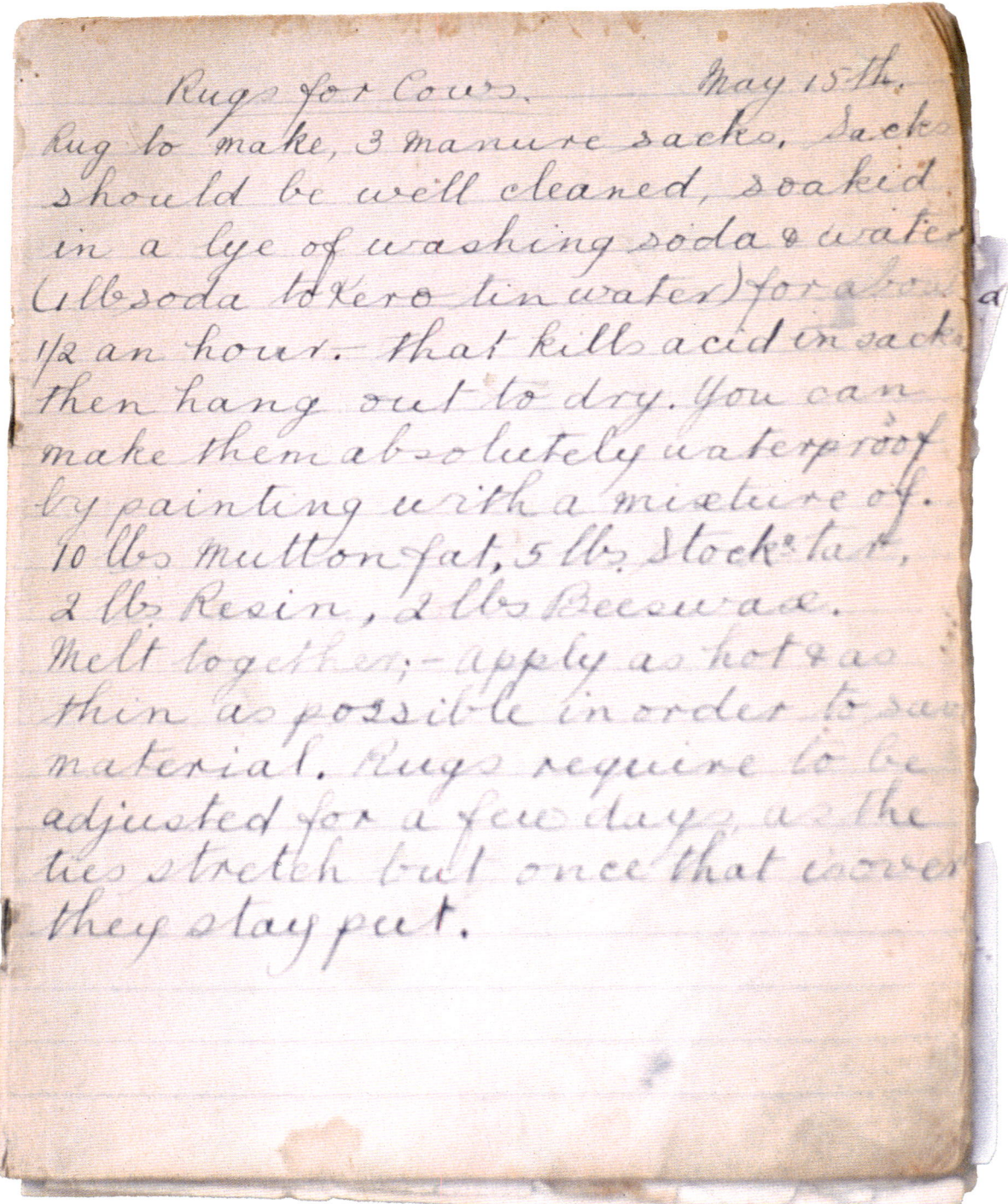

Rugs for Cows.                    May 15th.
Rug to make, 3 manure sacks. Sacks should be well cleaned, soaked in a lye of washing soda & water (1 lb soda to Kero tin water) for about a 1/2 an hour. that kills acid in sacks then hang out to dry. You can make them absolutely waterproof by painting with a mixture of. 10 lbs mutton fat, 5 lbs Stockm. fat, 2 lbs Resin, 2 lbs Beeswax. Melt together;- apply as hot & as thin as possible in order to save material. Rugs require to be adjusted for a few days, as the ties stretch but once that is over they stay put.

Handwritten instructions for making a cow rug kept in the Pioneer Women's Hut, Tumbarumba, N.S.W.

## KEROSENE TINS

Flattened tin was an extremely important early building material. Many people still recall early childhoods spent in primitive conditions in houses where one or more parts were composed of tin. Kerosene, so widely used in lamps before electricity, came in tins that could be cut, opened and flattened in many ways. They became shiny tin chimneys like scales of a reptile. They were used as walls, and even occasionally as roofs. The ways of recycling kerosene tins was only limited by the degree of imagination of their owners.

Old kerosene tin buckets are still found occasionally in country barns and sheds.

During the impoverished years of the Great Depression, kerosene tins reached their height in popularity. The wooden case as well as the tin can itself were the building materials of the time. Entire houses could be made of flattened petrol cans and most of the furnishings for the house could be made from the boxes.

Petrol and kerosene tins were usually 4 gallons in capacity, and came packed in cases. When filled with water they weighed 40 pounds. When no scales were available, they could be used as a rule of thumb when weighing things. As well as petrol and kerosene cases, many other cases were used to pack butter and cheese and were always in demand, if not for carpentry use, then as kindling for the fuel stove in the kitchen. Mrs Maidee Smith, who grew up on the

Western Australian wheat belt during the Depression, has described the furniture made from these cases that she had as a girl:

> "In our sleepout we had a chest-cum-wardrobe made from petrol cases, over which Mum had carefully pasted brown paper — using flour and water paste. There were three boxes on each side on edge, about three feet apart and the gap had a rail across for hanging our dresses. That was all right when we were little but we eventually grew out of it and hung our clothes in a wardrobe. The space in between then filled up with other things."[9]

Empty cans and tins were put to many uses. Dipper or tin mug from Kangaroo Valley, N.S.W.

Homemade egg bins could be found in many pantries. These were petrol tins with the top cut off and a wooden lid specially made for the top. Eggs were preserved rather than refrigerated. They were packed in "waterglass" or a greasy substance was rubbed into the eggs and then they would be placed amongst bran in the tin. They would keep for months this way. Tins could also be cut in different ways to make useful containers and utensils. Baking tins could be cut from petrol cans by slicing a few centimetres from the long side keeping the corners intact. The other part of the tin would be used elsewhere — perhaps as a feed or water trough for chickens. Petrol cases made good bedside tables as well as chests of drawers and they were invariably used as extra seats at the table for visitors. Tins were used as milking buckets, for carting water or cut down, they could be used as scoops for wheat or oats when feeding animals. Maidee Smith recalls using them "to carry a bucket of tea to the men at work in the paddock. They were just everywhere". At the back door by the tank a visitor would find a cut down tin for washing hands and faces. In places where water was scarce this would always be saved and tipped on to precious plants near the house or verandah. In many early photographs it is clear that kerosene tins were also used as flower pots. In some homes petrol tins or kerosene tins were used as washing up troughs. Few of these early gems remain. Butter boxes were a favourite. If they were not burnt as deal and were in good condition they could be made into footstools or seats. They would be covered in cretonne, the top padded with wool or rags and the edges covered with gimp tacked over the join. Baby clothes were often kept in such lined boxes and strips of leather could be used as hinges.

It was the universal practice in the first homes of selectors and settlers throughout Australia as well as battlers late into this century that produce bags, kerosene and petrol tins, boxes and crates would be kept, reused and remade. Commonly spoken of as the Australian tradition of "making do", it was also a matter of pride — of putting everything to good use, and of thrifty handling of the resources provided.

Petrol or kerosene tins and their cases were also used as feeding troughs for animals. Maleny, Qld, 1900–10.

Kerosene tins used in the home. Left: bucket, centre: breadbin, right: drawers.

SEWING

After the day's housework was done, often by the light of a candle or a kerosene lamp, a woman would rest by the fire. With the children asleep, she would proceed on the daily tasks of mending, sewing and darning. If there was any time left, perhaps a little "creative" needlework could be done — a floral motif on a pot-holder, perhaps, or a crocheted collar or edge on a milk jug cover. Very few poorer working women of the bush had the time to undertake the elaborate lace that was so common amongst their sisters in country towns and cities.[10]

Violet Trundle uses her Singer sewing machine while her daughter Ailsa embroiders beside her. Sewing machines were one of women's most important domestic objects and were handed down to their daughters. Hughenden, Qld, 1920s.

The first sewing machine was invented in America by Isaac Singer. The Singer Manufacturing Company established an agency in Sydney in 1865. This was one of the few inventions immediately adapted in the bush. Young women in the house learnt to make curtains, children's clothes, underwear and even winter clothing.

This extract from the 1910 diary of the widowed farmer Elizabeth Tierney who lived in Eurunderee, New South Wales, reveals the pleasure that the arrival of a sewing machine could induce:

> "*Tue 15* Very windy & Cool, I, Leo & John went to Mudgee, sold £1 worth fruit. Mr Davis & Mr Hourn, Singer Machine agents called while I was out. They left a machine for a few days & they taught the girls to sew. Ferdinand Muller called in for a few minutes, Jim Rheinberger went home. Katie & John went over to Mr Elliotts.
> *Wed 16* Fine day, Katie & Retta went down to Johnies after tea, Ferdinand & George came home with them.
> *Thu 17* Very Windy, Mr Hourn Singer Machine agent came & took the machine back, which he left here. Jim Buchlotz & others got a grand reception in Mudgee."[11]

The importance of the Singer sewing machine continued through the 20th century, and it became one of the essential tools for setting up a home. A woman might not inherit the land that she had slaved so hard over as a daughter, but she could be assured she might lay claim on her mother's Singer sewing machine.[12]

## DOMESTIC SERVANTS

The women who settled Australia as wives of selectors or smaller landholders were seldom privileged enough to have the extensive domestic help that the more affluent gentry expected.

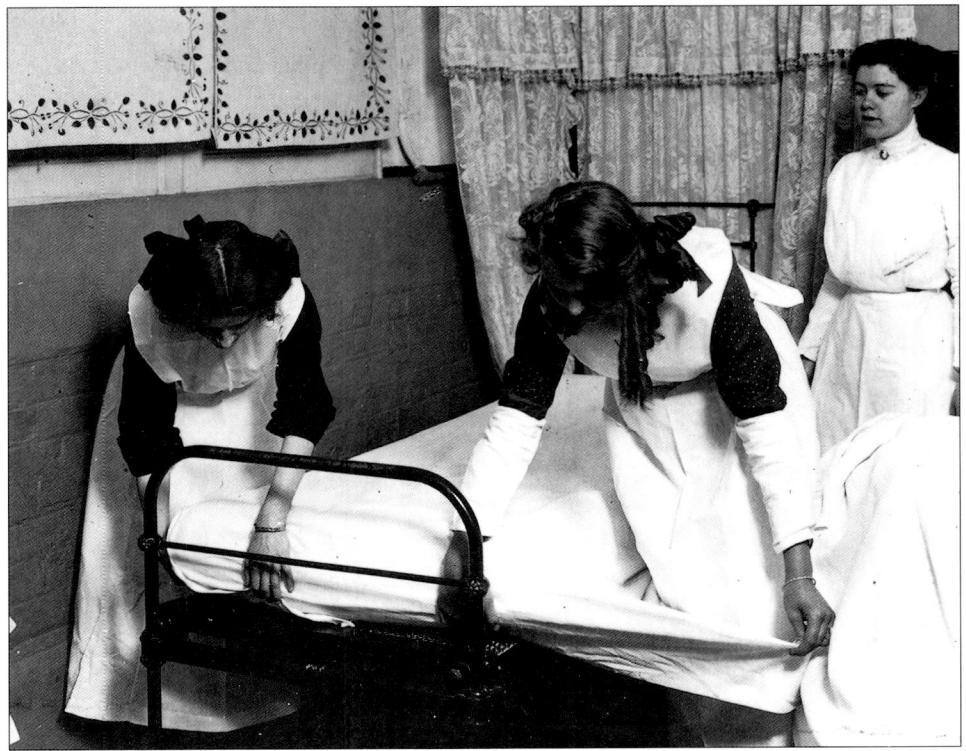

A domestic science lesson in progress. Young girls learnt the correct way to fold sheets under the corners of the mattress.

Mary Piety, a young Aboriginal girl who, before her marriage, worked as a housemaid with the Corkhill family in the Tilba Tilba district of New South Wales, c. 1898.

A rare photograph of an Aboriginal maid at work ironing, Cobar area, N.S.W., c. 1912.

The difficulty in acquiring servants was a common cry of 19th century life:

"It is true that though woman must, in every English home, play an important part, it is not in 'the bush' a prominent one. Her domestic duties are so engrossing, that if she had the power she has scarcely the time to stir abroad; of society, as we understand the word, there is little or none. The management of her household affairs requires constant attention, and the difficulty of finding tolerable servants, especially female servants, and of keeping them when found, reduces her to perform offices to which she had previous been unaccustomed."[13]

While women in the bush or outback might not employ the full range of domestic servants: housekeeper, parlourmaid, cook, scullery maid, kitchenmaid, head housemaid, lady's maid and children's nurse, they frequently sought assistance with washing and childminding. Initially girls of what was called "the servant class" were imported to Australia in large numbers to fill the employment gap. In Sydney young girls were educated to be servants in the "Female School of Industry", while in Adelaide "The Convalescent and Servants' Home" was opened in 1862.

Some accounts indicate the tremendous supply and demand gap that existed at the time. When a ship arrived advertisements would be placed in daily newspapers that the servants were arriving at a certain hour. Ladies then gathered eagerly at the depot questioning servants about their skills and offering advantageous conditions.

> "Extremely amusing it is to see a fair girl of Erin who has but a few weeks left her 'native isle' and the pigs and bogs behind her, surrounded by three or four of the ladies of Adelaide, each one out-bidding the other for Biddy's service."[14]

Hundreds of women used the Servants Home as their first refuge in the new colony and in one year, 1865–66, many of the 557 women who arrived in Adelaide took up positions as servants in the country or soon moved from Adelaide to Victoria following the boom of the gold rush. Many of such women quickly married and moved to selections of their own.

Trainee domestic servant at the Cootamundra Girls' Home, N.S.W., 1923.

In outback areas Aboriginal women often helped with domestic chores. Pictured are Fred Price (husband of Isabel Price, see feature page 26) and an unnamed Arrernte woman who worked at the telegraph station.

The household work required of servants in the new colony, although often hard and dirty, was excellent training for young women about to set up their own households in difficult circumstances in log cabins and bark houses.

The class differences between maid and mistress were well defined from the outset, although numerically, servants were few.

Children who were wards of the state were also put into service. In the early 19th century, children would be apprenticed or licensed out to employers even if they were under 16 years of age. They were expected, if in care, "to live with a duly authorised person". Such children who were boarded out often encountered difficult conditions or cruelty.[15]

It was common for young Aboriginal girls taken into "care" as wards of the state to be sent into domestic service. In many states the inspectors or protectors acting under the infamous Aborigines Protection Acts would visit the "girls' homes" and ask the older ones if they wanted to work:

"He'd find you a job: 'Would you like a job out in service? There's a lady wants a girl for service.' She might be in Meekatharra, but if she wants a girl to help her, well, that girl would have to go. She'd have to go there and work. If she didn't want to go, she'd still have to go."[16]

79

Mrs C. Williams at work in her kitchen bottling jam and preserves. Women in isolated circumstances learnt how to preserve and store produce until the next crop or harvest.

# FOOD

W herever selectors, settlers, or newcomers began a new life, providing food for themselves and for their family was a constant preoccupation. The need to transport goods in bulk over large distances meant that for much of the year daily meals were made from basic ingredients of flour, sugar, meat and tea. The combination of these and the quality of the repast varied proportionally with the enthusiasm and ingenuity of the cook. From many records of the first wave of European settlers it is clear that family food was greatly improved by the addition of wild meats, fruits, greens, roots, nuts and herbs. This was possible only through interaction with Aborigines and most often between the woman of the household and the Aboriginal women with whom she came in contact.

## DAMPER

For many people today, the smell of eucalyptus leaves, blue smoke hazily rising from a camp fire, billy tea and hot damper with butter and syrup bring warm and nostalgic thoughts of childhood and meals in the bush.

It was necessary, from the first, to cook a basic staple bread in the fire without the aid of an oven. Writing as early as 1850 Henry William Haygarth describes the staff of life of the interior as "a sort of cake, peculiar to the country and known by the discouraging appellation of 'damper'". He gives a reasonable description of its making but comments disparagingly "At best it is very inferior to bread and I presume that its prevalence has arisen from its being used of necessity in the long journeys and overland trips throughout the country, where it would be impossible to make bread".[1]

Stockmen developed the technique out of necessity. They were often away for weeks with only the camp fire to cook on and sacks of flour as stores. Most probably they had observed that many types of seed and nutbreads were made by Aboriginal women in the camps they passed.

The damper made by most European women was simply flour, salt and water, although sometimes a rising agent such as bicarbonate of soda was added. In northern Queensland, other ingredients such as coconut milk were included from time to time. Flour was first thoroughly kneaded with water and a fire made which would provide copious quantities of hot ash. When the dough was ready all unburnt coal and embers were swept aside leaving only the clear hot ash. This was opened out leaving a hollow in the middle to receive the dough. The damper dough was pressed out into the shape of a flat round cake several centimetres high and about 30 centimetres across. This was then laid carefully in the hollow and completely covered with ashes. After a certain time the ashes were swept away and the dough turned. It was then covered again and cooked through. For travellers damper was the ideal staple. It could be mixed by the roadside on a piece of bark, on a stone, or even in the flour bag itself by punching a hollow in the flour and pouring in the water.

Numerous variations of damper have developed since including Johnny Cakes — the small dampers about the size of scones which are cooked on a hot plate. These could also be fried in fat or dropped into boiling water. They are then known as "sinkers".

Mrs R. Wharton sifting flour to make a cake. Drouin, Vic., 1945.

Old camp ovens remain in many country homes. The meals they produced could be delicious but there was an art and technique to the preparation of the fire and the timing of cooking.

## BAKING

The universal "oven" was the camp oven — a heavy iron pot with three short legs and a flat lid. It had a handle and could be suspended above the fire or placed in it with ashes or coals laid on the lid for an even heat. Sometimes the oven itself was actually placed in a hole in the ground. The heat inside was retained by covering it completely with ashes and coals. This gave a very clean, well-risen dough. The disadvantage of these ovens, however, was their weight and the difficulty of maintaining even heat.

> "Of all the perverse, *iron-hearted* culinary utensils that were ever invented a camp oven is the worst. Coax it as she might it would either turn out the loaves mere sodden masses of dough, or else, from pure obduracy, would burn and blacken them to a cinder — ruffling the temper of the unhappy baker to such an extent that she was fain to wish the whole concern 'at the bottom of the sea'. The lid alone was enough to try the patience of Job, for no sooner was it raised with considerable difficulty, from its weight, by hands never very muscular or strong, on to a level with the oven itself, that it would tip over in nine cases out of ten . . ."[2]

Camp ovens were universal cookers of pioneer Australia from about 1855, however, the American stove, an iron cooker with a fixed range and hot plates, was small enough to be easily transportable. It needed no brickwork or fixing — you simply set it down in the fireplace, collected some wood and lit a fire. Australian manufacturers quickly followed this example and were soon producing a range of Colonial Ovens. Metters Bros, for example, produced a range in sizes designated by the length of wood each would burn. Some settlers built their own baking ovens outside the kitchen from handmade bricks and clay.

Many recall the delightful smells of baking which issued from their cavities. Children would be sent to collect quick-burning bark or tinder to heat the ovens to the high temperatures needed for baking. Skill in using wood is still important in some country homes where fuel stoves remain by choice:

"Baking day was another event. Mother didn't have a stove. She had a huge oven of brick and stone which Dad had built for her. On baking days we were sent to collect quantities of bark from dead red gum trees. With these we stoked the fire inside the oven until the bricks began to glow. Then the fire and hot coals were drawn with a homemade scraper, and the big tins of dough were pushed into the place where the fire had just been. The result was bread with an even deep brown crust. There has never been anything like it in my experience."[3]

Each type of oven had its special starter. Colonial Ovens were mostly started with "deal" or light timber. In the desert area spinifex or quick-burning wattle was used. In the high country near Tumbarumba, New South Wales, even into the 20th century, children still carried out the same tasks, using apple gum bark for a starter:

"Mother cooked in camp ovens and saucepans. On baking days Garney and I would take a chaff bag and go to big apple trees (apple gum trees always shed their bark) and get a bag full of bark for mother to cook her bread and cakes. Father made her a mud oven. Sometimes she used that."[4]

Iron fountains were kept on fuel stoves to supply hot water from their brass taps.

A miner's family outside their slabstone and bark house at Lithgow, N.S.W., late 19th century. A clay oven can be seen on the right.

## MEAT

The culinary legacy of meat and bread remains strong in country areas, supplemented by homegrown vegetables.

Alyce O'Donnell recalls the family meals at their properties in northern New South Wales from the 1920s to the 1940s :

"We had mutton three times a day — chops, cold meat and a joint for dinner. The first day's breakfast was always lambs fry. Dad often had bubble and squeak as well. In summer Dad would put the meat cut up in a big dish of coarse salt, rub it well and then put it in a sugar bag that hung from the ceiling and the liquid would drip through the bag into a dish at the bottom. The meat would be used straight from the sugar bag. We lived on corned, boiled meat for the rest of the sheep."[5]

Accounts from most areas agree. In the first year the O'Reilly family settled in the Green Mountains of Queensland, all they ate was corned beef, damper, potatoes, onions, golden syrup, tea, sugar and salt.

Coolgardie safe. The bag walls were kept damp. Any air circulating would therefore keep the food inside cool and fresh.

Meat had to be preserved due to the perpetual problem of heat and flies. Although techniques of salting, drying and smoking were widely known, sometimes, however, the heat and the flies won and if an animal was killed too far from the house, the meat would arrive home already "blown". Some cooks devised ingenious techniques of restoring meat to palatability. Rubbing the surface with vinegar or soaking the meat in vinegar removed the slimy surface and also took away the smell. Some women recall their mothers soaking the meat for days or leaving it in a running stream. Others packed it in brine, but

Jessie March prepares to hang a newly butchered carcass in the meat safe. Werrimull South, Vic., c. 1936.

the most common method was to treat it with salt or hang it in salt as "corned beef." Sometimes if meat was too salty there was a reason:

"There were a great many flies about and while it was being cut up they got at it all over and it was brought to us in a state that made us shrug our shoulders . . . after a careful investigation of each separate joint and a thorough washing of some of the worst, I salted it and put it into the tubs, and I am glad to say the only inconvenience we suffered, was having to eat meat rather salter [sic] than usual, for I thought it necessary to salt it well."[6]

## PIGS

For some settlers, particularly those of German background, pork replaced mutton and beef as the main meat in the diet although it should be said that pigs were popular with people of English and Irish background as well, with bacon being a favourite meal.

German settlers first arrived in South Australia in the 1840s and moved to the Barossa Valley where they set up extensive settlements. At first, life in the new country was extremely harsh. One group took three months to travel 40 kilometres to their land, walking all the way, carting their goods with them. Hunger was a real problem and so when life improved a little women took up all the old skills with joy and enthusiasm when preparing and processing pork.

Early kitchen implements.

The ubiquitous camp oven.

The killing of an animal was a communal event and a ceremonial social occasion. The Swiss and northern Italian settlers of Victoria also held regular gatherings to slaughter a bullock or pig. Each family member took part in preparing the meat. Pork or beef would be mixed with herbs, garlic, preservatives, wine and onions and squeezed into intestinal cases to make sausages.

Several elderly settlers from the Tumbarumba area recall the uses of a pig in detail.

Mrs Stuart explained the making of black pudding: About half a litre of blood would be collected from the pig. After adding approximately 2 tablespoons of salt, the mix was then stirred constantly "until the pig stopped kicking". This would prevent clotting. The blood would then be set aside for the final cooking. The pig's cheeks, flaps, ears and kidneys were then cooked together with half a cup of rice, pepper and herbs — thyme or marjoram. This meat was finely minced and added to the blood. The mixture was then forced into runners about 30 centimetres long, the ends of which were tied together to form a circle. To prepare the runners, the fat which holds them together was first stripped off carefully. They were thoroughly cleaned out, washed in salt water and turned inside out, washed again and then left to soak in salt water until needed so that they would remain soft. Turning them inside out was an art in itself. One end was tied and then water was run through gradually so that it could be forced through the other section. The stuffed circular runners were then dropped into boiling water for about 20 minutes. When cold they were threaded over a broom handle and hung in a cold place to keep.

# THE MATTICK FAMILY OF GUNDOWDA STATION

## BURRENDONG, NEW SOUTH WALES

These photographs depict family life at Gundowda, a sheep and cattle station near Burrendong, some 40 kilometres from Mudgee in New South Wales. The station was established by William and Herbert Mattick, two brothers who had emigrated from Bristol, England, in the mid-1800s. They commenced work as jackeroos around Mudgee before starting off on their own. In 1881 William married Angelina Suttor and they had five children. Among them was Walter Mattick (b. 1898), who eventually took over the property, and his sister Olive (1895–1979).

The farm proved prosperous and the family was able to build a handsome homestead with marble fireplaces, a splendid dining area and five bedrooms. Walter then married Marie Maraun.

When Marie arrived at Gundowda the role of women on the property had changed dramatically. Although Angelina Suttor, William's grandmother, had worked extensively with the cattle while the farm was being established, Marie and her sister-in-law Olive mainly worked in the domestic sphere. Housemaids helped with cooking and housekeeping. Washing was done in a copper set on a wood fire, using homemade soap. Domestic chores included carrying wood, cleaning fireplaces, scrubbing boards, baking bread and making jams .

The women were all keen on shooting. Their targets were usually rabbits or crows that were pestering the sheep. Recreations included weekend visits to neighbouring homesteads where they might go swimming or play tennis.

The Suttor family photographed out shooting on Gundowda Station in 1918.

## THE PIONEER

BY NANCY HOWARD

Long ago in a rough, slab house
Dwelt a woman of noble heart.
She toiled each day to rear her sons
And helped her man on the cattle run.
She rode side saddle, with babe on her knee,
Chasing scrubber cattle in the wild country.

One little whim which brought her wealth —
A minor act in the Commonwealth —
Was to collect dead wool, left by the males,
Cleanse and bag it, then render at sales.
Her final reward was just six bob.
Her only reward for a tedious job.

Along came a tramp, gaunt and hungry.
She fed him damper, corned meat and tea.
Noting his boots were battered and wet
She reached for the jar where her wee horde was kept.
"Take this," said she, "it will help a fraction."
And there you have — Christianity in Action.

Poem by Marie Mattick's daughter, Nancy, about her great-grandmother, Angelina Suttor.

Marie Mattick with four of her children and the family car, c. 1927.

Milking on Gundowda Station, 1928–30.

91

CHICKENS

Keeping chickens was often difficult but rewarding. In areas near wild bush, they had to be fenced extremely carefully or foxes would attack. Although they were prized primarily for their eggs which improved baking enormously, on occasions women would reluctantly have one killed. Chickens, or "chooks", were really the woman's concern and were regarded with great fondness:

> "I also devoted many hours to the well being of a large number of fowls, ducks and geese, and a great amusement they were to me, so much so that I was on affectionately intimate terms with every cock and hen and members of the feathered tribe on the premises, having known them from the eggshell. The worst effect of this friendship was that I could never make up my mind as to which of my favourites I could best part with and sacrifice for dinner."[7]

Most families kept a few chickens for eggs and meat. The women and children were generally responsible for feeding them. Photograph taken in Queensland, c. 1910.

Feeding the chickens. Keeping them in many bush areas meant perpetual vigilance as foxes would attack at night. Photograph taken at Northcliffe, W.A., 1945.

## RABBITS

Thousands of rabbits invaded many country areas in the late 1890s. Trapping rabbits, therefore, became a common occupation. Carcasses were sent to Sydney where they were sold for up to 10 pence a pair. Sometimes in "rabbit drives" as many as 500 would be caught. The 1890s were difficult times, the first of several depressions in Australia. In rural areas drought badly affected wheat crops. An unfortunate result of drought was that stock gathered around the few waterholes left in dried up creeks. They would become bogged and die there so that the water was spoiled. Some settlers even had to rely on this water supply — boiling it and then filtering it through charcoal. From this period to the close of the Depression years rabbits became the most important secondary meat in country districts, yet because they had become a scourge, they were considered the food of the poor.

Selling rabbits at Moruya, N.S.W. Rabbits provided an important meat source as well as income from their skins.

Young children help to stretch rabbit skins. Tumut area, N.S.W., c. 1947.

Hunting rabbits at Guyra, N.S.W., 1929.

Rabbits spread in plague numbers destroying many properties. Shooting rabbits became a necessity undertaken by both men and women. Photographed in 1947 at Northampton, W.A.

In order to keep up appearances, many could not admit to eating rabbit:

"My mother used to make a very nice rabbit stew, and I was writing a letter to one of my aunts and I said 'We have had our troubles during the year' — I was imitating the older people. And my mother said 'You must *never* tell people about your troubles. Take another piece of paper.' Then I said 'We had rabbit stew for dinner.' . . . '*Never* tell them that we ate rabbit!' "[8]

During her childhood in the 1914–18 war, Beatrice Elliott recalled that she would set traps and nets over rabbit holes each evening:

"We never used to let the dogs go with us because if they would catch them, you see, they would tear the skin. Well, if the skin was torn it wasn't worth much. But that's what we used to do — skin the rabbit. Charlie, my brother, used to go and skin them and put them on this wire frame and hang them out to dry. There was a sort of an Indian fella . . . Afghan fella. He used to come in and call and pick them up. Every month he used to come. Well, the more we got, the more money we got . . . if anybody wanted something it took a lot, you know, Mum used to make a lot of things, but it took a lot when they've got a big family . . . We were always independent, you know, be careful not to waste. Of course, Grandma — she was a very saving woman, Grandma was, and she wouldn't waste a thing if she could help it. Well, I think I followed her suit because I'm just the same."[9]

# Jane Kell

## (nee McIlroy)
## 1851–1931

Jane Kell was the daughter of William McIlroy and his wife Julie (nee Hines) who emigrated from Ireland to Australia in 1851, the year of her birth. The young baby Jane was left with maternal grandparents at Moygallen, Galway.

At six, Jane came to Australia in the care of a nurse to join her parents and lived at various times of her childhood at Warrnambool, Port Fairy and Hamilton in Victoria. Her parents had six other daughters and two sons.

Before marriage, Jane was brought up to observe all the niceties of life. She went to a small school at Warrnambool, where she had to curtsey to the mistress and present a penny for her tuition. Later she became a tailoress.

In 1884, at the age of 33, she married a station manager, Robert Kell, and went to live at Burtundy Station on the Darling River, New South Wales. The family recalls it being a very large property. The Burtundy homestead was made

Jane Kell, c. 1884.

of slabs with an iron roof. It had brick chimneys and a wide verandah, wire-netted against rabbits.

In the 1890s supplies to these remote properties on the Darling River had to come by steamer up the river. Jane would order well in advance and look forward to receiving large sacks of flour, sugar, rice, 40 pound boxes of currants and raisins, salt, vinegar, spices and pepper for preserving, as well as the essential kerosene for lamps.

The main staple meat was mutton, and goats were used for milk and cheese. Jane baked bread in a brick oven and kept tallow to make soap and candles, as did so many pioneer women. The family recalls that a Chinese gardener grew vegetables on the river bank, but no fruit trees were yet established.

Jane Kell had one child, Walter Andrew William, born at Wentworth in 1886, whom she educated at home herself. As the only white child for many kilometres he became very close to the Aboriginal families on the station. He had an Aboriginal nursemaid and playmates and could speak their language. He was called Oonda-narka, which meant "countryman of mine", because he was born there.

The station required some permanent staff — cook, overseers, stockmen, as well as Aboriginal workers. Jane made most of the clothes, utilising her skill as a tailoress. The family kept chickens, and feathers from poultry were used to make soft pillows for the family.

In Jane Kell's papers there is evidence that she was prepared to try a great many other foods than the boring and monotonous salted mutton or beef. There were recipes for wild duck, kangaroo tail soup, and cakes from swan's egg. But the family never ate rabbit!!

In the 1890s along the Darling rabbits built up to plague numbers. Combined with droughts, this caused bankruptcy and eventual sale of the property.

By 1904, things had improved — Robert was managing a sheep station in the Hamilton area. Photographs of this time show a homestead with flower garden, potplants on the verandah as well as notes and cuttings to help Jane with her housewifely tasks — *The Australasian*, *Woman's Budget*, *Home Notes*, recipes for cakes, puddings, white-wash and medicine.

Throughout her life Jane Kell typified her generation and was never idle. She loved cooking and although she lived with her son and daughter-in-law in later life, she made sure she did the baking — cakes, biscuits — as well as the jams and pickles. Her large dresser was always full of pickled onions, walnuts, chutney, tomato sauce, Worcestershire sauce, mushroom ketchup, plum sauce and mixed pickles. She still made her soap in a kerosene tin on a wood stove with fine white sand brought from the river bank by her young granddaughter. She mended and patched on her old sewing machine, worked by hand and knitted all the socks.

Her knitted and crocheted laces were worn on petticoats and embellished doileys, tray cloths and tea cloths in her own home and that of her descendants. She kept meticulous patterns and died in 1931, aged 80.

Jane Kell (centre) and her sisters wearing velvet jackets sewn by Jane.

Jane and Robert Kell at Burtundy Station on the Darling River, N.S.W. The overseers and Aboriginal staff are also pictured. A rabbit plague along the Darling forced the eventual sale of the property.

# FRUIT AND VEGETABLES

Most families sought to supplement meat and damper with vegetables. Stinging nettles would be boiled and even the stems of pumpkin leaves could be stewed and cooked in a white sauce. Children always had to "have their greens".

Fruit trees and a vegetable garden were usually immediate priorities along with completing the house. Precious seeds were brought on long overland journeys or exchanged with travellers who might have brought a small bag of fruit with them.

Enterprising women organised garden plots close to the house. Most recall that their sons or husbands would dig the garden in which they would plant the seeds they had kept carefully. In dry or arid areas melons and pumpkins were the most readily grown vegetables.

As water was precious everywhere the vegetable garden was seldom grand as even small plants grown close to the house had to be hand watered — often with leftover washing up water. But many succeeded, particularly when galvanised iron was widespread and rainwater tanks the norm. A little could always be spared for the vegetables.

Once the fruit trees had grown it was soon time for preserving and bottling so that fruit could be enjoyed out of season. Nothing was ever wasted. Fruits were bottled, or made into chutney, and citrus was made into marmalade. Melon jam became a ubiquitous country favourite. In forested areas blackberries were seldom regarded as the scourge they later became, but more as delectable pickings for young children. If they were plentiful they would be brought home and made into jams or pies.

A large vegetable garden beside a timber hut in the Gippsland area of Victoria, c. 1884. Photograph held in the Australian National Gallery.

Janet Lachlan at Portland, Vic., in the 1930s. The well-fertilised cabbage beneath her bird's perch has outgrown all its neighbours.

# Clara Elizabeth Ellen McNabb

## (nee Birkin)
## 1882–1955

Clara and Frank McNabb together with Clara's brother Harry Birkin and his wife, Edith, were among the first selectors in the rough mallee area of north-western Victoria. They became small farmers concentrating on wheat, sheep and small livestock. Clara's domestic creativity, her love of gardening, cooking and animals, as well as her flair in adapting to her environment are well remembered.

The McNabbs were granted a 259 hectare block of land — Block 46, Parish of Yatpool, situated 8 kilometres south of Yatpool railway siding on the east side of the Melbourne-Mildura railway link. Frank McNabb arrived at the block on 29 April 1913, and finding the survey pegs, cleared a small area in the centre of thick mallee bush where he pitched the tents. Frank and Clara lived in these tents from 1913 to 1917, as Frank cleared the block. They then brought an existing weatherboard house by train to Carwarp and put this on the cleared block. Clara assisted in the carpentry on their new home and at one stage in 1918 she won a nail-driving competition at a Mildura Traders Picnic in the Carwarp Recreation Reserve.

The rooms of their new house were lined with hessian, then newspaper, then wallpaper. However, mice ate the flour paste used to stick the paper down, so this was later replaced with plaster.

Clara McNabb in the sheep pen. The walls are made of grubbed-out mallee roots.

Clara looked after the vegetable and flower garden, fed the family pets, milked the cows, separated the cream, looked after the pigs and kept a large battery of chickens. The garden Clara developed was remarkable — a complete cottage garden within mallee root walls. She grew full-sized pepper trees from peppercorns and, close to the water tanks, a marvellously productive currant vine.

There were many aspects of wheat farming in which Clara was involved. She sewed the wheat bags with hanks of sewing twine for freight and storage. These rows of bags would wait in the paddocks to be sewn and carted; for this she wore a leather pad in the palm of her hand secured by short lengths of string. She also treated the wheat for smut by turning the handle of a barrel in which the wheat was mixed with fungicide powder.

Clara and the children also took on the task of stooking sheaves of hay. They had to be stood upright on their butts to dry. She and the children assisted by cutting the bands of every sheaf before Frank fed the hay into the chaff cutter mouth.

Clara was remarkable for her love of animals, both wild and domestic. She had an instinct for inventing cures for their ailments; she found she could prevent tick fever in her chickens by coating their perches with kerosene. At one time Clara kept a pet emu named Matilda, which she fed on bread and milk and for a period she had remarkable peacocks. She reared many pet lambs and loved her cats.

Her domestic life was typical of her pioneering generation. She baked quandong tarts with fruit from the many wild trees on her selection. Her kitchen was a large, warm living area where the family gathered. Her loneliness was alleviated by the close family companionship of her brother and sister-in-law who lived nearby.

She brought her charcoal iron with her to the mallee and regularly boiled the clothes, then transferred them into a wooden barrel in which she used her dolly to remove the mallee sand. With her Singer sewing machine, she made hats and bedcovers in green Indian Head and all manner of practical items from sugar bags.

Clara's walled garden was a haven in the dry mallee area of Victoria. She adopted wild animals including "Johnny" the joey. Pictured 1938.

Clara with her pet cats Stiffy and Sandy sitting outside the cream-separator shed.

Clara at the gate in the mallee root wall.

Home and garden at Carwarp, 1925.

Yabbying at Auburn, S.A., c. 1913.

The fate of this harvest of wild birds is not known, but many rural families relied on game and birds to supplement tedious rations.

## WILD FOOD FROM THE BUSH

Nature itself offered the most interesting variations to the settlers' diet. Sometimes these were predictable — substitutes for meat in the form of kangaroo, wallaby, wild birds or wild ducks. Some settlers, however, interacted far more closely with the local Aboriginal population and as a result were adventurous and experimental in their diet.

Wild honey was always popular — the honey bags or cones could be put in water to make honey mead. Older children would be sent out to a particular hollow tree when they knew there was a beehive inside.

Billy cans or pannikins of the honey were brought back to the house as a slushy mass where mother would hang it in fine calico produce bags with a dish beneath. The syrupy liquid would then pass through the gauze leaving a clear, fine, glowing honey to be stored in jars for the family. But these were rare occurrences compared to the numerous tales of other attempts to use bush food.

Kangaroos and wallabies were widespread and many were shot by the early settlers. Some parts of the meat would be cured, the rest would be eaten fresh. Kangaroo tail soup or wallaby tail soup is one of the few well-known recipes showing the culinary experimentation of this era.

The harvesting of a kangaroo meant that often visitors would call by to share in the party repast. The native dish of the Van Diemen's Land bush was called "a steamer". By repute it was a delicious hearty meal. The most tender sections of kangaroo meat, free of tendons and fibres, were carefully cut off and chopped fine. Some pieces of salted pork were added to this and the whole was put to steam slowly over the open fire. The tail of a kangaroo was most often quickly roasted whole in the ashes, after which the fur would be scraped off carefully. It would then be sliced through and fried with flavourings to hand — onions, mushrooms and herbs being the favourites. Wild mushrooms were always enthusiastically gathered whenever found as they added flavour and excitement to the meal.

Many unusual native animals were eaten by early settlers — wombats, possums, koalas, swans, goannas and freshwater crayfish or "yabbies". Sometimes the settlers reveal a slight twinge of regret at seizing the opportunity to eat beautiful wild birds:

> "Coming home I spied 4 black cockatoos chattering in a bush hard by. I fired and killed one . . . I've since thought that there was something like cruelty in what I did. It was like slaughtering in cold blood. They were so vulnerable in their ignorance and innocence that never having heard the report of a gun before. However these thoughts did not trouble me at the moment. I took the birds home and gave them to my wife to make a pie of. The children said it was a pity to kill such pretty birds, but we ate the pie, nevertheless, with a good deal of relish, although I had a slight twinge of conscience when my mind reverted to the sight of the birds chattering joyously in the scrub."[10]

A kangaroo shooting party in Western Australia at the turn of the century.

Not so widely understood perhaps by subsequent generations was the importance of wild fruit and green vegetables to the first wave of settlers. They had the opportunity to learn processing and cooking from Aborigines and to know the things they tasted were not likely to harm them. By the 20th century, although outback women were often living in similar physical circumstances, their small areas of land were near cattle runs and large areas of country had been cleared completely of its native bushland. The Aboriginal population had been forcibly dispersed and the traditional foods were no longer available.

In her childhood reminiscences, Mrs Fairfax Conigrave wrote of annual visits to the peninsula on Hindmarsh Island, to gather a fruit she called "montrees". These grew on creepers across the sand.

"It was about the size of a black currant but had the smell of an apple, therefore, it was called native apple. 'Montree', I suppose, was the blacks' name for it. For a considerable time we had no other fruit, except water and pie melons; the former made very good marmalade and the latter very passable pies, if made properly, which I will say my sister Jane knew how to do. The montrees made very good jam."[11]

Such expeditions were great fun for children leading remote pioneering lives with their parents. For many, gathering wild foods was work and an important aid to family health and survival.

> "We regarded the gathering of the fruit as work, and hard work, too, because we had either to kneel or stoop to pick them up. Some seasons they were very prolific, therefore if we got to a big creeper we were not long in filling our baskets, which gave us more time for cockling. No sooner were the baskets filled, and placed in the boat, than off we would go, helter-skelter, over the sand hills, up hill and down dale, to see who would get on the beach first. Then off would come our boots and stockings, and with our skirts tucked up, in we would dash. Oh, the fun of it!"[12]

Numerous other wild fruits and green vegetables were spoken of by early settlers. Waterlily roots, or corms, were eaten as were wild yams, particularly in Victoria where many enjoyed the delicious murrnong — the root of a wild daisy. One of the most popular and well-known varieties of fruit was the quandong — a parasitic tree which has rather tart fruits the size of small plums, usually red in colour. It has a large seed or kernel from which oil was sometimes extracted.

Wild quandongs remain a delicacy in arid regions.

> "One evening I discovered the quandong tree growing on the banks of the Darling, which is rather an uncommon locality for this shrub to be found, preferring, as it does, the arid plains beyond . . . After filling a sack full, we returned to our camp; it was, I remember, just under one of the hills forming Dunlop's Range. I made some very good preserves in the evening, which we all approved of."[13]

In Queensland the favourite native "fruits" were the rosellas — the flower heads of a species of hibiscus. The fruit is a purple-red colour and the outside long leaf or husk is actually petals which enclose the seedcase. The fruits were gathered complete with their flower petals before they had opened. The calyx could be used on its own. The seed pods also have a sweet, tart flavour. The rosellas were poached, stewed, used in pies and other desserts and in drinks, jam and jelly.

A carrier and passengers on the old Ballarat Road, Vic., c. 1860.

A camel-drawn buggy at Eucla, W.A. Afghans and Sikhs were important traders and carriers.

# SHOPPING LONG DISTANCE

T hroughout the country settlers secured their provisions in different ways. For those along main routes only a few days travel from large towns, the essential flour, tea and sugar supplies would be bought in bulk and the wait might not be more than a few weeks. However, families in remote areas had to rely on their ingenuity when ordering goods in large quantities.

As towns grew, country stores emerged. These stocked the basics, but when they ran out their customers had to wait until the next bulk delivery either by rail or by wagon. Catalogues sent from large stores, either in the city or country town centres, were immensely important in country areas. It was possible for a woman in fairly remote circumstances to select elegant goods for her home and arrange for a forwarding agent to have them sent to her district. Such catalogues that exist today provide a marvellous repository of information about prices, styles and fashions throughout the decades. This form of long distance shopping has remained important in country areas well into the 20th century.

## AFGHAN CAMEL TRAINS

In central Australia the large "Afghan" camel trains brought supplies only twice a year. In the Centre these Afghan "immigrants" were essential to the early settlers. Although the train line eventually replaced the great camel routes, initially it only went as far as Oodnadatta and the camel trains would collect the goods at the railhead and transport them into the interior of the country, stopping along the way at bores and finishing at the town of Stuart (now called Alice Springs).

The Afghans were misnamed by the Australian settlers they came to work for. In fact, the early immigrants originated from the area now known as Pakistan and northern India rather than Afghanistan. The "Afghan" immigrants were responsible for opening up the Australian interior from 1860 to about the 1920s. Their great camel trains were eventually superseded by the expansion of the railway throughout the continent.

Only flimsy evidence remains of the women who shared the lives of these men who came to Australia. As they were British subjects the pastoralists who sought their service and imported the camels had no difficulty in arranging for the men to travel to Australia, but immigration restrictions prevented them bringing wives. Many therefore married young white girls in Australia by contractual arrangement. Many also cohabited with Aboriginal women. There is evidence that such spouses were often "bought" as was the custom in India, in a simple contractual arrangement in which the families were paid in exchange for their daughters. In some cases the wife's mother and siblings would live with the family.

Such marriages placed the women in most unusual and poorly understood cultural situations. For most it involved leaving their home and joining the Moslem community. The religious observances concerning the role and behaviour of the women of such communities are probably the reason why so little remains in evidence of the thoughts, feelings or behaviour of their wives.

Although the Afghan children led free and unrestricted lives this altered significantly for girls when they entered their teens and so the photographs that

Early immigration laws prevented Afghan men bringing wives and therefore many married white women in Australia. This photograph of Mr and Mrs B. J. Dervish was taken outside their home at Marree, S.A., c. 1910

Afghan children in South Australia, c. 1910.

remain are mainly of young children. Women seldom had any contact with the camels or went on the long treks but kept to the homes within the tightly knit community.

Some of these early travellers were in fact not Moslems but Sikhs, clearly distinguished by the name of Singh. Roddah Singh, for example, was a well-known Sikh in the town of Marree. The South Australia Directory records him as a carrier residing in Marree from 1930 to 1940. He had 70 or so camels but with advancing age he could not work the large camel string so used only a few to do occasional hawking.

Most Afghans worked camel strings and serviced the arid interior of the continent throughout western New South Wales, the north of South Australia, central Australia, western Queensland and deep into the Northern Territory.

In the 1920s there was consternation among larger landowners over what was termed "the camel problem". Camels were increasingly running wild and damaging property. A Camel Destruction Act gave pastoral landowners the legal power to shoot destructive animals. For the communities of Afghans at the railheads whose livelihood depended on the animals the effects of the Act were ruinous. Grazing fees were increased and many "scrubbers" (wild camels) were shot leading to the demise of the camel transport trade.

The laden camel train of Ali Mohammed arrives at the Stuart Arms Hotel in Alice Springs.

Greeting the camels at Roxby Downs, c. 1910.

*Above and right:* Women posing with camels. Between 1890 and 1900 in Western Australia.

In many areas travellers stopped to pose and be photographed astride or at least seated on these remarkable animals.

## HAWKERS

In the latter part of the 19th century, and early 20th century, hawkers' vans were a common sight in the more settled areas. Their appearance was always a cause of great excitement as word travelled from home to home that the hawkers were coming.

These itinerant hawkers were mainly Sikhs, travelling in vans pulled either by camels or by horses, loaded with a variety of hardware. The Sikhs originated in the Punjab and observed a strict code of behaviour, based on their strict military background and close historical association with the British Raj. They were the elite. They wore turbans as did the Moslems, however, theirs were differently constructed. Each Sikh also wore a single silver band around the wrist as a symbol of Sikh fraternity. The names of the Singhs remembered by early pioneers are numerous — Roddah Singh of Marree, Kaser Singh of Farina, South Australia, Bhagwan Singh who fought in the Crimean War and kept a medal given to him by Queen Victoria, and Sunder Singh who worked with a van in the Bute and Tickera districts of South Australia.[1] In the Wagga area

Cher Singh and his hawker's van by the side of the road near Wagga Wagga, N.S.W.

The travelling draper's van of Mr A. Whittenburg, South Australia, c. 1925.

of New South Wales, Cher Singh was a well-known local supplier. In Queensland, Bernard O'Reilly recorded the excitement the family felt in their pioneering days when Jundah Singh "came with his van full of secret sliding panels and drawers containing goods that were, to us, comparable with the riches and mysteries of Jundah's native India".[2]

The great Afghan camel trains carried the goods in massive bulk — vast sacks of dry foods, building materials and station equipment; the smaller hawkers' vans and wagons contained a multitude of different items needed mainly for the household.

Jack Miller of Lankeys Creek, New South Wales, recalls locals saying that Cher Singh used to come to Lankeys Creek carrying a basket on his head well before the 1920s. Later he had a horse and cart and he and other hawkers would occasionally sit around smoking bubble pipes. The Sikhs had a burning ground or crematorium at Lavington.[3] In the same area, Minnie Galvin recalls that her mother "bought dress material, sheeting, calico, socks, needles, cotton, scissors, tape, sardines, pens and anything she wanted" from the Indian hawkers:

"Garney always took one old Indian a jug of milk. He gave Garney a pencil for it. There was always lots of opium poppies growing around our house. When they were in seed, one of the Indians always asked could he have a bunch. Mother let him take as many as he wanted."[4]

While the hawkers provided remote households with essential drapery, pots and pans, and clothing, the difference in culture meant that they were the first to be suspected of evil intent, particularly by women in remote situations whose husbands were away a great deal. The daily prayers offered by Moslems to Allah, their keeping to themselves, their distinctive foods and preference for curries and hot spices, as well as their dress and skin colour, fueled early European settlers' tendencies towards ethnocentrism and racial bias. The lives of the women who chose to live with the Moslem and Sikh immigrants became tainted as well, although in the "Ghan" towns of South Australia the relationship was one of acceptance.

Camels were more important than horses in ensuring that families in remote areas received supplies of food.

Where fear was not present, the visit of a known and friendly hawker was always anticipated with excitement and pleasure. The treats that they offered and the chance to replenish essential implements were greatly appreciated. Although mothers might have filled the shelves of their pantry with many jars of jams and preserves, to children, the new, the foreign, or the mass-produced product that came out of a tin with a pretty label was like a gift from another world.[5]

Hawkers collected goods from main distribution points and would then take their vans or wagons out to stations or towns along well worked tracks. They carried bolts of cloth, clothes, haberdashery, sewing needs, lollies, chocolates, pots and pans, tobacco and cigarettes.

In outer areas of country towns and cities, where distances remained a problem, hawkers replaced their historic use of horse and camel with vans and many women today still recall the early hawkers' and tinkers' vans that were a welcome sound in the local areas. One such van is preserved intact in the Birdwood Mill National Motor Museum in South Australia.

The trip to town to the general store was planned well in advance.

## VISITS TO THE GENERAL STORE

Many country settlers did not head into the bush with the purpose of farming the land — often the more successful set up businesses supplying workers on the goldfields, or farmers and others with the necessities of life. These "general stores" were everything their name proclaimed them to be — catering for all the settlers' needs from medicines and foodstuffs to saddlery and clothes. They carried pots and pans, haberdashery, spices, cutlery, candles, bullock chains, yokes, wheelbarrows, brooms, nails, castor oil, starch, pickles, snuff and tobacco.

Nineteenth century stores were mostly operated as a family business, the storekeeper's wife being as essential as the storekeeper in the daily routine. The store owners, like publicans, were often the social centre and focus of country life.

A baker's shop at Gulgong, a goldfields town in New South Wales. This building is of bark with a wooden facade.

Shops flourished on the Western Australian goldfields but businesswomen such as Miss Murray, tobacconist and stationer, were rare.

Many storekeepers were generous but others made sure of their profits at the expense of the under-capitalised selectors. Cash loans might be provided occasionally but interest was often charged. In the mid-19th century for example, Steele Rudd describes his father's first harvest of corn selling for £12. Much earlier, in 1845, the prices in a store in South Australia showed how little £12 would have bought to keep a farm going: candles 7d; castor oil 5s a pint; buckets up to 9s each; leather gaiters up to £1 a pair, bullock chains 10s; bullock yokes 10s 6d; wheelbarrows 12s to 28s each. The essentials of life like wheelbarrows, leather gaiters and bullock yokes could therefore take up the entire proceeds of a harvest. As the selectors were usually in debt to the storekeepers, they had little to spend each time.

Trips to town to stock up on provisions were well planned. A shopping list had to be prepared days ahead to ensure that bulk buying was efficient. Forgotten things would have to be done without until the next trip into town, sometimes weeks away. The general store served the community as a social centre and the storekeeper's advice would be sought on everything from farm machinery to patterns for clothing. Women would arrange to meet their friends and neighbours from outlying districts and keep abreast of local news at the same time. For children it was indeed an exciting day as the buggy was harnessed, best clothes produced, all having been washed carefully and laid out the day before. The thought of lollies and sweets for the first time for weeks would be foremost in their minds.

The excitement and lure of the country store extended well into the 20th century and even those who grew up in the 1940s recall the delights around the walls. The store was often first a slab hut and later a sturdy timber building. Its walls held ropes, kerosene tins, equipment for horses, boots, sturdy workmen's shirts and farm implements. In another section of the store the food was displayed — tins of biscuits with exciting labels, jars of sweets, and behind the counter, tins of treacle, mustard or tobacco.

The trip to town not only took in the country store, but other necessities of life as well — this was the opportunity to visit the bootmaker, a milliner, a cabinetmaker or builder, and perhaps the chemist shop or furniture store. In 1882, the South Australian town of Noarlunga for example, had a baker, blacksmith and farrier, boot and shoemaker, butcher, wheelwright and coachbuilder, an inn, and a post and telegraph office, although frequently in smaller towns the general store would also double as the post office.

## THE WILLUNGA STORE

*If you want the very best of goods*
*Delivered at your door,*
*And at the very lowest rate,*
*Deal at the 'Willunga Store'.*

*If it's curtains for your windows,*
*Linoleums for the floor,*
*Blankets, sheets or counterpanes —*
*Try the 'Willunga Store'.*

*If it's clothing for your little ones,*
*Hat, dress or pinafore,*
*Boots or hose, to warm their toes —*
*Ask the 'Willunga Store'.*

*Suits made to measure — guaranteed,*
*Gents' hats of felt or straw,*
*Ties of many shades and price,*
*At the 'Willunga Store'.*

*They keep dairy produce of the best —*
*Once tried, you'll ask for more,*
*Oats, chaff and bran you always can*
*Get, at the 'Willunga Store'.*

*If you need a cooking range,*
*Pick, hammer, axe or saw,*
*Posts and rails, wire, tacks or nails,*
*Try the 'Willunga Store'.*

*Horses and traps, let out on hire,*
*Farmers are catered for.*
*They're Agents for Farm Implements,*
*At the 'Willunga Store'.*

*They're stocked with everything you need,*
*From ceiling to the floor,*
*If you deal there, you'll find them fair,*
*At the 'Willunga Store'.*

ETHEL ELSIE JACOBS[6]
1911

Bell & Macauley's corner store in Drouin, Vic., 1945. It carried pots and pans, crockery, glassware, gardening equipment and preserving outfits.

The kerosene crate comes in handy as Nurse Pearson baths baby Lorne in outback Western Australia.

Barefoot children of the bush.

# CHILDBIRTH, CHILDHOOD AND SCHOOL

As many 19th century women had extremely large families, the risks of childbirth were multiplied many times over. In remote country areas a midwife usually attended the birth. These were renowned older women of the district, many of whom had nursing training but more often operated on wide first-hand experience. A great many were legendary for travelling large distances in the dead of night to deliver a baby. There were very few doctors available in the outback areas, so the business of having children was entirely women's concern, although if complications arose, the family would attempt to transport the woman to the nearest hospital.

The subject of childbirth was never discussed in front of children. In letters women would refer to pregnancy or stillbirth simply as "troubles".

The older children were expected to take the younger children well away from the house, or the husband, if he was home, would perhaps deploy them in a creek bed with enough fun and games for the day while the midwife attended his wife in labour. Sometimes the youngest children were very insistent and had to be restrained or told stories to prevent them running to their mother whom they could see was in some distress. At other times the children were simply forbidden entry to their parents' room.

As a child, Coral Starke lived an itinerant life, moving with her parents between Barooga and Dandenong in Victoria to Moonta and Jamestown in South Australia. She recalls her mother having children at home just before the 1914–18 war.

> "Yes, all her children were born at home, with an old midwife. I can remember the old midwife at Barooga coming out, and she liked her little tipple, you know. We'd be all sent off on a picnic or somewhere for the day, and when we came home the baby would be there, but it would never cross our minds to ask why, and I think that might've been the only rest my mother got, because you was kept in bed for ten days during those periods. Mum enjoyed that, I think."[1]

The district nurses who worked in remote areas in the early part of this century were among the many unknown heroines of pioneering days. One nurse, Miss Kathleen Waterhouse, recalled working in the Riverland area of South Australia in 1921 and 1922.[2]

The family snapshot bears the caption "Sydney and Bremer Shaw in bathtub on pond with duck".

The district nurse had to be "ever ready". Miss Waterhouse had a room in the bank with a window that opened on to a verandah. Messengers would tap on her window any time, day or night. She would often travel to outlying patients on the maintenance trolley along railway lines. They would be powered by a worker or a relative. Working conditions were far from sterile.

> "We had no sepsis at all in amongst the midwifery patients, and I'm afraid I didn't expect it either. Because the air was cleaner . . . and soap and water can do wonders. [She always carried a load of old sheets and linen] because they wouldn't have anything prepared as a rule . . . you had to make do with all sorts of things. And for my own sterilisation I had a kerosene tin cut in half this way for the big instruments and cut square ways for . . . the smaller instruments."[3]

One particularly stressful incident that happened while Miss Waterhouse was nursing in the Riverland area has stayed in her memory for six decades.

> "This was the Riverland area itself and it was one of the hotels. I was sent for about midnight . . . I was brought over to one of the domestics in her room and she'd had a miscarriage, and the foetus was there about this big, you see. She wouldn't own up that she'd had this till I had to show her what she had passed. The foetus was there so I said 'You *were* pregnant; so you might just as well be truthful about it.' But the mother of the lad which was the one son of the house, who was known to be very free with all the girls, as a matter of fact the girls used to say they didn't dare to go out with him, which was probably very responsible for this, and she came to me before I left in the small hours of the morning, after cleaning everything up and having everything in buckets — yes, that was another thing . . . it was dark when I got there, and there were men camping out in the back yard . . . no woman came to assist me in any shape or form, not even any of the other maids came near me — and then the mother — the wife of the man that owned the hotel came to me before I left and said I wasn't to say *anything* to *anybody* about what had occurred and I was not to try and get rid of *anything* from the room on their property. I had to take it away and try and get rid of it anywhere I could."[4]

All alone, the rather distressed Miss Waterhouse went to great lengths to dispose of the foetus clandestinely in the middle of the night. She calls this a "horrific experience" but even today her concern for propriety prevents her from divulging the name of the family or of the son involved in the incident.

Until relatively recently the experience of many young Aboriginal women in outback reserves and stations on becoming pregnant was vastly different to that of a white pioneer woman. The following account is from a stockman's daughter in Western Australia. Like many Aboriginal girls, she was brought up in homes and lived part of her life as a domestic servant before moving into the general community. Many became pregnant at a very young age, and their babies in turn were placed in the care of the state.

> "There was a lot of girls at Moore River, had been out to service, different places they were at and they misbehaved themselves out and they'd get pregnant. Well, they'd put them back in Moore River to have their babies. There was one big dormitory. the mothers' ward, where they'd stay till they had their babies. No one else was allowed to go there. They'd stay twelve months and then if they was lucky, they'd get another chance, if someone was willing to take the mother and the baby."[5]

Elizabeth Cox, a renowned midwife of the Richmond River area, N.S.W.

Annie Maria Harlow, pioneer midwife of Blackall, Qld.

The stories of many midwives at the turn of the century are remarkably similar. They were strict, somewhat fearsome, wore black and rode magnificent horses long distances at night to attend patients.

## CHILD MORTALITY

The incidence of child mortality from contagious disease in the 19th century and early 20th century is well known. Death of children had a profound effect and although the families were larger the love and loss of children is recorded eloquently in many women's diaries.

Women in isolated situations might call on the midwife to assist in funeral arrangements or undertake this themselves. It was very common for mothers and close friends and relatives to prepare a child's body for burial, decorating it with flowers and observing other important symbolic gestures of love and remembrance.

# MARY JANE COBDEN

## (NEE GRIFFITH)
## 1854–1927

Mary Jane Cobden was a midwife of the Rosewood Humula district in southern New South Wales. Her grandson, Mr John Cheney of Humula, has recalled details of her life for the Pioneer Women's Hut historical records.

After marriage at 16 to John Cobden, an ex-Crimean war soldier, the couple lived for a few years on the Ballarat goldfields, then travelled to Mannus by horse team, and then to Bells Creek near Rosewood, where they settled. Later they moved to another selection on Umbango Creek, south of Humula, finally settling at Rosewood. Mary's husband died in 1896 and as she was then the mother of ten children, she turned to what she knew best — midwifery.

She had only one horse, a black mare, which she rode sidesaddle to her patients in all kinds of weather. She crossed many swollen creeks in thunderstorms to deliver a child. Mrs Cobden's notebook records that she delivered 91 babies between 1900 and 1923. Each birth is recorded briefly including the baby's weight:

"Madge Annabella. Born 30 of April 1914. Born 12 O'clock in the day Monday morning. Weighed 7½ pounds Malabo Park Malabo near Wagga Wagga."

Nurse Cobden rode "loose" so she could travel overland faster. She strapped two ports (bags) and a sugar bag to the side of her horse. In one suitcase was a change of clothes, in the other a rug. The sugar bag held her midwifery implements and her little black notebook. A bottle of Lysol was always included in her medical gear, and scales to weigh the baby.

Like many other midwives of the period Nurse Cobden often stayed on to do the housework and washing. She also nursed the dying and laid out the dead in a coffin. She covered many areas — Westbrook, Umbango, Tarcutta, Humula, Downfall, Forest Hill, Tumbarumba, Rosewood, Carabost, Tooma, Book Book, Kyeamba, Little Billabong, Garyowen and Oberne Station — sometimes travelling up to 80 kilometres.

Stories of Nurse Cobden are often colourful. In one she was assaulted on a lonely ride by a youth whom she knew. Her response was to say she would tell his mother — far more of a penalty and deterrent in a small community than punitive action. After this incident the police allowed her to carry a revolver.

The following poem was written inside Mrs Cobden's diary to deter her patients' children from stealing it.

*Steal not this book for fear or shame*
*For in it is the owner's name.*
*When you die the Lord will say;*
*"Where is that book you stole away?"*
*And if you say;*
*"I never stole that book."*
*The Lord will say;*
*"My dear friend, the gallows will be your end."*
*So don't steal it!*

No one dared, and this poem perhaps ensured the survival of her records today.

A child's funeral, South Australia, c. 1850. Grief at the loss of babies and young children was a part of many women's lives. Laying out the body was most often undertaken by the women of the family.

Children who fell victims to infectious diseases were isolated. If possible, they would be sent to a hospital such as this, the Subiaco infectious diseases hospital, Perth, 1919.

Mrs Emily Churchward recorded the death of her three-year-old daughter, Violet, in 1883:

"Mother and Clara came to help me, for the patients became delirious, and Violet, worse than the others, was quite violent at times. Her throat grew worse, and became paralysed so that she could not swallow, and wasted almost to a skeleton . . . There was little we could do for her . . . Our dear one left us on February 22nd. I gently closed her eyes and the mouth which was beginning to smile, saying from the bottom of my heart, 'Thank God' her sufferings were over. . . . Then I washed her hands and face, brushed her hair and changed her nightdress. I laid out our kangaroo skin rug on the drawing-room sofa, covered it with a sheet and pillow, and . . . with our neighbour from across the road, carried her in and gently laid her down."[6]

Mrs Churchward then recounts how she gathered pure, white carnations with a pink edge, and placed them in her daughter's hands, and put a wreath of pure white flowers on her head and another on her feet, laying her in a white coffin.

In the memories of Mary Boothby about the disappearance of a three-year-old daughter of a shepherd, a most tragic event is related.

Mary Boothby was a lively young woman of English birth who married a South Australian grazier in 1864. They lived at the tiny settlement of Tintinara.

"During the summer a sad event happened to one of the lonely families who lived in the distant out-lying huts on the border of our run, about 10 miles from the head station. The father being one of the shepherds was of course away with his flock from sunrise to sunset leaving his wife and five little ones alone."[7]

This family lived in a small hut and most of the time the children ran wild, although the eldest boy, who was 9 years old, helped his mother by chopping wood and fetching water.

". . . there came a day when the three little ones were playing round the clearing which was near the hut. The mother thought she could hear the little voices all the time, but when she went to the door with her baby in her arms to call them in to supper only the two elder children of five and seven years appeared, and when she asked 'Where was Annie', the girl of five answered that Johnny had put her down a wombat's hole. . . . Johnny however stoutly denied the accusation and the anxious mother ran out loudly calling the child's name.

Poor Annie was but a baby, scarcely three years old, so the mother took slight comfort in the thought that if she strayed away she could not have gone very far in the short time since she last seen her running across the grass with a rabbit clasped in her arms.

Nothing could she see however and no baby voice came back in answer to the loud terrified calls of her name. . ."[8]

The father on coming home with his sheep, learnt of the tragedy and in desperation, tired after the day's tramping, headed to Mary Boothby's station, where her husband agreed to take action in the morning. He organised a search involving every available hand in the vicinity, and they scoured the area, digging up every wombat hole they could find. Tragically, they had no success, and the young child was never found.

At the turn of the century a favourite children's pastime was to harness the pet billygoat to a homemade cart and set off on imaginary journeys. These billycarts came in all forms, from well-constructed buggies with full rig to tin trays or kerosene boxes on wheels.

Human "kids" or other four-legged pets sometimes substituted for the patient goat.

# ELIZABETH McCALLUM

## (NEE TAIT)
## 1831–1903

Elizabeth Tait was born in Peebleshire, Scotland, in 1831. In 1850 at the age of 19 she married her cousin John McCallum and they emigrated to South Australia on the *Reliance*. Both Elizabeth and John had become experienced shepherds during their childhood in Scotland. On reaching Australia they began working for their uncle, Adam Borthwick, who owned a property called Mikkira in the area of the Eyre Peninsula. In those days, before the fencing in of sheep, the flocks had to be continually watched. In many parts of Australia there was a shortage of competent shepherds.

John and Elizabeth earned a wage of about 25 shillings a week.

The McCallums eventually took out selections by themselves and they built a dwelling called Wholla Hut. Although a simple building, consisting of two roofed sections connected by a walkway, it

Kate McCallum (b. 1870), surviving daughter of Elizabeth McCallum, pictured with the family car and children Doreen, Nell and Scal.

was, by all accounts, a happy and friendly place. The lively couple, who retained their Scottish accents all their lives, received a constant stream of travellers and visitors. Even when entertaining complete strangers, they would never charge for their hospitality. One of their Scottish neighbours, a Mr Brown, was a favoured visitor. He would notify Elizabeth of his arrival by playing his bagpipes as he neared Wholla Hut. She would know to put on the kettle.

Between 1852 and 1870 Elizabeth gave birth to 11 children. She appears to have accepted childbirth as an extremely routine matter. A visitor to Wholla Hut reported one morning that he had heard crying during the night. Elizabeth, who was busy over the stove (it was her custom to provide each man with six fried eggs for breakfast), explained that "Yes, we had a bonny wee boy born in the night". He replied that surely she should be resting. Elizabeth said that she would do so, but not before she had cooked breakfast. While Wholla Hut provided a base for the family, the McCallums appear to have led a fairly nomadic lifestyle. Birth records show that nearly all Elizabeth's children were born at different locations on the Eyre Peninsula. In 1860 alone, John McCallum took out four separate leases.

Besides running sheep and dairy cattle, the McCallums were industrious gardeners. They planted mulberry trees, carob bean trees, figs, almonds and a great variety of vegetables. They grew wheat and barley as well, sowing the grain by scattering it from a bag tied around the waist.

In 1872 the McCallum family was hit by great tragedy. Their eldest son, John, who had been boarding near Port Lincoln where he was going to school, contracted diphtheria. His mother went to nurse him but he died and she returned home. Scared that she might be harbouring the disease she removed and burnt her clothes as she approached Wholla Hut and bathed herself in the creek. The precautions were useless, however, for she was already carrying the sickness although immune from it herself.

It was not long before several of her other children had come down with the symptoms. She harnessed up a dray in order to dash back to the nearest doctor at Port Lincoln. On the way they passed Maggie and James, two of their children who had been minding sheep at Yunto Well. Their father yelled out to them not to approach for fear of death and that they were not to go back to the hut. For several months the only communication between Maggie and James and their parents was by shouting over a wide gap.

By the time they reached Port Lincoln, the children were fatally ill, an epidemic was raging at the time and there was little that the doctors could do to alleviate the situation.

Dr Phillips, who carried out a parliamentary inquiry into the tragedy, reported the McCallums' situation on reaching Port Lincoln:

"On their arrival they were located in a hovel, and, I am informed were all lying together on the floor. This treatment certainly would not have a beneficial tendency. They were, however, shortly after removed to a better house, and, in every way, were better circumstanced; notwithstanding they died. A boy about 16, and a girl little over 20 years of age, recovered; these, with the baby who escaped infection, are all that are left of 11 children."

Although it seems beyond comprehension how Elizabeth and John managed to cope after losing eight of their loved ones in a single month, they persevered in their management of the farm. Elizabeth had a new baby girl in 1873 and another boy in 1876. Around this time her husband began to go blind. He became confined to Wholla Hut and Elizabeth ran the farm by herself. She died at Wholla Hut in 1903. Her life had brought incredible hardship and suffering. She was truly a heroic pioneer.

The McCallum's shearing shed at Wholla Hut, Tumby Bay, S.A.

Elizabeth McCallum recorded the births and deaths of her children in her bible. The bookmarks were made by the children.

## EDUCATION AT HOME

The education of young school-aged children was always a difficulty for isolated families. The solution was either a home-based education or long distance travel to school. For many, there was simply no choice. Either the mother, an older sibling or a family relative undertook the children's education at home. Lessons were often sparse and held in the hours of day when the children were not otherwise required to assist in farmwork.

The majority of remote outback women had to undertake the education of their children alone. In many cabins, either in the cool shade of the verandah on a homemade desk or in a busy kitchen in the midst of the cooking or cheese making, mothers supervised their children. They taught them to read and attempted to give them the rudiments of education which would equip them for the world beyond home. Itinerant visitors helped. Mrs Hilda Freeman recalls life in the Murrumbidgee area of New South Wales, in the 1860s:

Alison Ashby being instructed by her Aunt Meta on the verandah at "Wittunga", Blackwood, S.A., 1906–07.

The governess on Angorichina Station, S.A.

"My greatest trouble was to get schooling for the children, for there was no settlement closer than Narandera. However, the gold fever had brought all kinds of people to the country and not always the best educated made the best advance. Usually some educated man could be found who had made a failure of his life, and he would be willing to act as tutor for a small wage. We were able to find a man who had tried driving bullocks, but was more fitted to teach children, so we gave him 10s per week and his keep. He did very well as a rule, but sometimes the longing for drink overcame him and he disappeared for a while. He lived with us, both at Wright's Bend and when we shifted to the river."[9]

Relatively few of the women featured in this book had the means to employ a governess, the traditional English way of coping with education in isolation. In fact, highly trained governesses were advised not to travel to the colony:

"Young women of the class employed in the National Schools of England and Ireland, able to impart a plain English education, and prepared to take situations with settlers in the interior, where they would have to wash and dress the children as well as to teach them, will generally marry well. But for the higher class of accomplishments there is no demand worth crossing the seas to meet."[10]

On larger properties children's labour was not essential. They were therefore largely allowed to run free apart from a few hours' schooling a day. But most had to undertake quite arduous work while they were very young. Both boys and girls helped with chores outside the house. In large families older girls were also trained to gradually take over the supervision and care of their younger siblings. As prosperity increased the expectations of girls diminished and, whether they liked it or not, lady-like leisured accomplishments of needlework and piano playing were encouraged, particularly in the latter decades of the 19th century. This century the more typical Australian outback girl was skilled in the ways of the bush, knowledgeable about plants, animals, tracks and some aspects of survival. She could often ride "as well as a first rate hand" and yet was mindful of the need to make items for her "glory box" in preparation for marriage.

As the years progressed the supply of newspapers and magazines gave country families access to information about the world. The wireless also played an important additional role in education at home.

In outback areas where the pioneering development of cattle and sheep stations has been a more recent part of Australian history, a feature of childhood was the interaction of white children with Aboriginal children. The stories of pioneer settlers of the Northern Territory, for example, intermingle and intersect the parallel story that Aboriginal families tell of their association with white settlers. Children were often minded by Aboriginal nannies during the day. They accompanied them in various activities around the house if they were employed as housemaids, milkmaids or shepherdesses. At times they also had the pleasure of going on bush adventures digging for yams, chasing goannas or collecting fruit.

Bob Laver versus the Hayes boy near the Stuart Arms Hotel, Stuart (now Alice Springs), c. 1920. (*See feature on Edith Laver, page 166.*)

The Ball children work on their correspondence lessons at "Lyndhurst", the family farm near Tambellup, W.A.

Mrs Ball made the desks from kerosene packing cases and taught her children all grades from infants to grade seven over a period of 17 years. Pictured from left are Lorna, Wilma, Verna, Una, Ivor, and Norma with the lamb.

Sawyer's Valley open air school, 1910.

One teacher school in rural Western Australia.

Maisie Robb gets a lift to school. She taught at the Aboriginal children's school, "The Bungalow" at Stuart (now Alice Springs).

Children of "The Bungalow", the Aboriginal children's school at Stuart, where Ida Standley (second from right) taught between 1915 and 1929.

## BUSH SCHOOLS

From the 1840s until about 1870 the number of schools in the colony varied and many were run by private individuals. Children did not have to attend. Between 1872 and 1895 all six Australian colonies passed laws claiming "free, compulsory, and secular education". This was a grand and hopeful claim yet poorer families still found it extremely difficult to provide their children with appropriate education. In the early decades of the 20th century there were many more schools and as the Australian population had increased dramatically there were not as many isolated families although the lack of schools still affected more remote settlers. Most often children walked to school or rode on a pony, sometimes several were seated together. Horses or ponies would be tied up outside the school and children were warned about riding with strangers. Reminiscences of pioneers who experienced life as a child in a country school early this century recall the earthen playgrounds where the single teacher, whether male or female, would earnestly attempt to educate girls about making flower gardens, and teaching the boys to grow vegetables.

Minnie Galvin recalls her school in about 1910:

"Our first teacher's name was Robert Kelly. Ours was his first school. He taught us drill and we had to march and drill every morning. At recess and lunch time he always played games with us. There were about 30 children going to school. They came from Carboona mine and all round. Our teacher taught us first aid, singing, how to recite poetry. The boys he took about a mile away down the creek and learnt them all how to dive and swim. He also made flower gardens for the girls. The map of Australia was the main flower bed. The boys had vegetable gardens. Later on when there was only 11 or 12 children going to school, he grew a pine tree for each child near the school. Our school was known as 'The Park' school."[11]

The interior of a chaff shed was set up as the temporary school at Wudinna East, S.A., 1926.

Exterior view of the chaff-shed school.

The residence of Mr H. E. Bannister where Ella Parsons boarded.

*Left*: The young teacher, Ella Parsons.

The pupils and teacher of Nungarin school, W.A., 1913.

Verandah of a country school, Holbrook area, N.S.W.

An older sister might have to take several younger children with her to school:

"I used to take the younger kiddies to school — one of 'em was about two and the baby was a few months old. I left the baby in the pram and the other one used to play in the playground that me father made for her. On the verandah it was, so she couldn't run away; I took a few toys for her. They had their lunch at dinner time, a couple of beer bottles of goat's milk (with a teat on top) for the baby, jam sandwiches for the two-year-old. That's what I think kept me back a bit at school; I've sort of taught meself a lot since I got married; I didn't get on so well at school."[12]

In many areas, boiling the tea billy was a feature of the daily life at the school. Just before lunch some of the boys would be sent out to make the fire and by the time lessons ceased at lunchtime the billy would be boiling. Every child drank a pannikin of tea.

Larger schools were coeducational although boys and girls were educated differently. School photographs enshrine this — boys on one side, girls on the other. Boys were taught mainly physical skills, while sewing samplers or work for the glory box occupied a large part of the day for girls, along with lessons on English history and readings from the Bible.

Apart from reading skills probably the best education such children got was from life itself, the Australian environment acting as the main teacher. Children interacted daily with all manner of birds, animals and reptiles which gave them an understanding of the country.

"Our playground was peopled with many small, grey lizards with dragon-like spikes from head to tail . . . One day, a huge black snake disturbed the 'quiet' of our lunch hour; Peg grabbed a willow stick and went to do battle, but the 'joe blake', as snakes are locally known, retreated under a pile of flood-drift between the great weeping willow."[13]

Such stories are commonplace along with memories of pets kept by the schoolteacher — cockatoos and galahs. The bush lore of how to cope with dive-bombing magpies in school playgrounds is a part of every country child's armoury. Numerous families also kept a retinue of wild birds and animals at home as pets, feeding injured or orphaned kookaburras, parrots, joeys and even goannas.

One problem confronting many women teachers sent to isolated areas was finding suitable accommodation. In theory this had to be arranged well in advance by the parents of school children. Sometimes, however, the materials for the school would not arrive before the teacher so the first schools throughout Australia were often held in all manner of structures — tents, barns, churches and halls, and very often under a shady tree.

The pay and conditions of female teachers were markedly inferior to those of men until relatively recently. The basis of this was doubtless the expectation that boys were saving for marriage and a home and would need to be the breadwinners and girls would one day get married, despite their undertaking

Morning tea for the children, mothers and teachers of the Gilliminning Rock school, W.A., 1907.

full-time careers as teachers. Yet it is clear that many young women who taught had dependent members of their families and a great many never married.

Education improved for children in remote areas with the advent of the wireless and more formal, organised correspondence lessons. Sometimes Sunday school teachers visited in wagons or carts.

Mrs Usher of Toowoomba, Qld, with her birds. Many country women were renowned for taming or nursing wild birds and animals.

Children at play, Port Hedland, W.A., 1900.

In many schools there were seldom more than 50 pupils. In 1877, Miss Margaret Hotchin began a day school in the Wesleyan Chapel at Wirrabara, South Australia. Although it was a non-denominational private school, the teachers still had to satisfy the government inspector of their standards of teaching. Visits occurred from time to time. The inspector's exams were the only yardstick for the promotion of pupils from one year to another. Unfortunately, education became something of a haphazard affair as many young children were kept at home to help with farm and household chores, and if they missed the exam, they were forced to repeat the year.[14]

Lessons included "moral", "object", and "temperance" as well as a number of crafts — ship carving, carpentry, brush making, boat making, bookbinding, wood punching, fretwork, clay modelling, plaiting and weaving, with great emphasis being placed on discipline and drill.

# BETTE BILTON

b. 1914

*Personal Reminiscences of Bette Bilton — Teacher, St Helen's Plains State School, 1941.*

"I was appointed as Head Teacher to open a new country school, my first year out of Teachers' College. The children had attended other schools in the district and some had received correspondence lessons. On the first day, the room, built by the farming community, was not finished, there was no furniture or equipment — just myself, the children and a few books that I had brought with me ... Gradually we were able to secure all necessary equipment — desks, table, cupboard and easel blackboard sent from the Education Department. The children came to school by horseback, and bicycles (in dry weather, as in wet weather it was far too muddy); cars bogged, as there were no bitumen roads. As teacher I had to ride a bicycle in dry weather, one and a half miles from the boarding house, through a paddock, and walk in wet weather. Around the road was over three miles. The school was in the corner of a scattered wheat farming area, on a plain with no trees or water. The children had to bring their own drinking water, until the rain came.

There was no post office, shop or bank — the only public building was the school which was paid off by holding euchre parties and dances in the school room on Saturday nights. All the furniture had to be taken out on Fridays, at first left in the open air, then I had to go back on Sunday, clean out the room and with some help, return the furniture ready to start school work on Monday. My salary was £6 3s 4d a fortnight."

Pupils ready to go home after school, 1941.

Bette Bilton and her pupils at St Helen's Plains State School, Vic., 1941.

Children at play, Alice Springs, 1920s.

Playing in the paddock on the old farm equipment after school, Northcliffe, W.A., 1925.

# LOTTE SULLIVAN

## *Reminiscences of a Saddler's Daughter of South Gippsland, Victoria.*

"In my childhood, I was the second of five children later to become eight, and when I compare life today with the early 1900s I would prefer to describe our existence as 'poverty'.

My father was a saddler, but my only memories of him was a very ill man in and out of hospital in Melbourne. We lived in South Gippsland. The only transport was a horse and vehicle — no made roads. The only doctor 10 to 12 miles away (again with horse and jinker), no telephone — only at the local post office 9 a.m. to 4.30 p.m. (also several miles away), axle deep in mud most of the winter, and replaced by dust in the summer. We wore lace-up boots — having one pair of shoes reserved for Sunday School, and every Saturday night the tub would be brought in for a weekly bath (only one small tank for water). We children would quarrel to be first for the bath, 'cos we had to share the water.

I recall one house we lived in had never been completed and some rooms had earthen floors. The kitchen was the main living room and had a kerosene lamp where we gathered to do our homework. In the winter, again we kids would fight for room to put our feet in the oven to warm them, before going to bed. Our bedroom lighting was a candle — and on extremely cold nights we each had a 'brick' heated on top of the stove — this was wrapped in newspaper and an old towel and put in our beds for warmth.

I also recall laundry day (which was every day — on account of five children, two parents and one grandparent and a limited supply of clothes). There was never a laundry in any house I lived in and always only one tank of water. We lived on top of a short steep hill (to avoid floods).

At the foot of the hill there was a 'spring', a natural supply of water, so with kerosene tins with handles and soiled clothes and linen, my mother would take us down to the spring and there between some bricks set up a fire and boil the washing in the kerosene tins. When washed she would often dry it on a nearby fence — much easier to carry up the hill when dry.

Entertainment was almost nil. On one occasion we had a hut near our house and my father would allow 'rabbit trappers' to live in it. Our big delight was to visit the rabbit trapper nearly every evening. Very often he would have a twisted cone of newspaper with boiled lollies or 'humbugs' and distribute them to all five of us. We were mainly dependent on Grandma (my mother's mother) who owned two cottages her husband built in Moonee Ponds (a suburb of Melbourne). When her rent letter arrived, we knew she would go shopping and would each in turn get something to wear — and also a luxury in the way of fruit.

Every Saturday night my hair was curled in rags, also my elder sister's was too. Another big thrill — my brother's getting a long straight sapling and erecting an aerial — for we had progressed to a wireless — and the very first sound that we heard — we thought we were among the 'elite'."

The Flying Doctor Service provided education to many outback children through the use of its radio equipment and the supply of receivers. School of the Air followed. Barry Coles is photographed taking lessons outside his family tent. His father was a well-sinker and moved throughout the Northern Territory.

## SCHOOL OF THE AIR

Although the children of remote families in the south-eastern states had access to assistance with correspondence lessons through various programmes on the "wireless" or the radio, it was not until much later that the children of outback stations, properties and small farms could receive the same benefits and assistance with their work over the air. The Royal Flying Doctor Service provided the mechanism for transmitting lessons to remote children from about 1950 and this opened up not only opportunities for education but friendship and contacts with the outside world in otherwise extremely isolated circumstances.

In Queensland the School of the Air was opened in Cloncurry as late as 1960. For the women on remote properties this was an immense and welcome help in the solitary task of educating their children.

Correspondence lessons in progress at Ballidu East, W.A., 1932.

## CHILDREN'S WORK

Raising large families was a mixed blessing for outback women. The early years were immensely physically draining with cooking, washing and caring for the children, a major part of the day. However, as the children grew, a hidden benefit emerged — they became useful and often contributed substantially to the family economics.

Older girls looked after the younger children, freeing their mothers for work in the home or to assist in the paddocks or yards beyond. Seven-year-olds could look after livestock — goats, sheep, ducks and chickens. They could also weed gardens and sort produce. Some helped much more substantially by cleaning and sorting in the threshing yards and the woolshed. At the turn of the century, young boys of very poor families would take a position on a neighbouring property virtually for their keep or for a small amount and board. Although the boy's own family lost his assistance, they did not need to support him and he might be able to bring some money home. Young girls helped their mothers with the arduous and difficult wash as well as the important chore of buttermaking — frequently an extra earner for the family. They helped parents cart produce to town and chased off pests and vermin from the crops.

Quite frequently the girls would go into service for a neighbouring family, either on a payback system or for a wage. In times of sickness in small communities this was often a charitable gesture but it would be reciprocated in times of need.

> "In 1916 our neighbour Mrs Wright became very ill and was put in the Corryong Hospital. Before she came home mother went along and did all the washing and cleaned up the house for her. Then when she came home Mum went to give her a further helping hand and it was decided that I should go and help her. I stayed with Mrs Wright for 12 months. During that time a young man and girl ran to our house, left his girlfriend in a sulky a few hundred yards away and asked Mum would she take the girl in. They came from Mannus and were on their way to Holbrook but the girl couldn't go any further. Mum took her in and the baby arrived shortly afterwards. The girl hadn't a stitch of clothes for the baby or herself. Mum was expecting too, so she gave the girl a lot of her baby clothes, nightgowns, powder, et cetera for herself."[15]

Most families prefer to remember the good times of childhood, the fun and games, handmade toys from tin sticks and wire, and the treats — parcels of prunes, biscuits or lollies occasionally ordered from far away.

> "I would make a pan of black toffee, of treacly sugar on Saturday night and this would be so much enjoyed that the children thought it worthwhile being good for the sake of the reward. The black, treacly sugar came in sacks, and often the treacle oozed out from the bag onto the floor. On Sundays, of course, we all had our weekly dose of sulphur and treacle."[16]

Aboriginal children branding a calf, Moola Bulla pastoral station, W.A., c. 1910–18.

Letting the horses drink.

Watering the precious green lawn.

In country areas children often helped substantially with the daily tasks. They fed chickens and animals and watered gardens.

# DOROTHY MAGUIRE

### Childhood in Kangaroo Valley
### 1852–1944

In 1944, Dorothy Maguire, the daughter of pioneer Kangaroo Valley settler Patrick Maguire, wrote the story of her hardworking childhood on the family selection of 20 hectares, in the 1860s and 1870s.

"At first the land was very heavily timbered forest and brush, well watered, a creek ran through the property, as well as numerous springs. Father's first job was to erect a shelter for us to live in, which consisted of slabs, and a bark roof and earthen floor. The hut completed we settled down to a life of hard struggle and toil.

Firstly, we had to clear the land to plant corn and potatoes. We had one cow to begin with. While the crops were growing we went on clearing the timber ready for more crop planting, which was very hard work as we were only children at the time, my brother

Edward being the eldest aged 15 years, my sister aged 13 and myself aged 10, the three younger being babies. My Mother also helped Father do the clearing.

We had much to contend with, for a start our tools were very primitive ... our only tools being a hoe, spade, one mall, wedges and brush hook. We made all the handles for our tools out of hickory ...

Our nearest store was 60 miles away at Wollongong. These trips were very trying. We had to follow the blazed track over the mountain as only packhorses were used and the journey taking three days to get there and back. Father only went every three months for supplies. On one of these trips Father bought a cross-cut saw and carried it on his shoulders all the way on foot as his pack and saddle horses were both heavily loaded.

As time went by we felled more timber and cleared more land for crops, burning-off the timber by rolling logs in heaps with the help of hand spikes. At the end of a heavy day's toil we looked more like black fellows than white children. We had no clock, having to guess the time by seeing the tree shadows turn around for 12 o'clock, and the hourly laugh of the jackass, called the settler's clock. There were no 44 working hours in our week. We made our candles in a mould with bees wax. Bees were very plentiful in the bush and we always had plenty of honey. There were a large number of cabbage trees and we made use of them. We girls picked the young leaves and bleached them white and made cabbage tree hats for the stockmen and ourselves at 1 shilling each, these were made by candlelight at night.

In the early years all our crops were chipped in by hoe. No easy work when it came to acres. Our first wheat crop was a failure, taking the rust, all our hard work was done for nought. However, we started again and chipped in 10 acres of wheat, non-rusting Egyptian type, which was a great success. Father paying 10 shillings a bushel to get the seed. We grew arrowroot, but unfortunately, no sale for that, so we fed it to the calves in the milk.

We grew our own wheat, thrashed it with a flail, ground it into flour, we also grew our own hops to make bread. In earlier days we had to live on damper made on the hearth and covered in hot ashes to cook. Later we purchased a camp oven, a three-legged pot, iron kettle and a tin teapot. As time went on our wheat ripened, we cut it with reap hooks and stacked it until required. Father bought a small steel mill and had to thrash the wheat with a flail and then grind it into flour. We also grew our own fruit and vegetables. We were never idle.

We still had much to contend with, crops failing, drought and bush fires which destroyed our fences, caterpillars, grasshoppers and floods. Snakes, hundreds of them, all sorts and colours — had many escapes. Father bought more stock and reared all the calves and they soon grew up.

There were no rabbits but many worse pests such as wallabies, paddymelons, bandicoots, native and tiger cats, dingoes, which played havoc with young calves, poultry and pigs. When the crops were ripening it was my job, wet or dry, to keep the birds off the crops. That meant running up and down all day to frighten them. That done, come home, turn into the stockyard

Dorothy Edwards (nee Maguire) in her later years.

as we were milking 10 cows. The blacks were very numerous but did us no harm ...

We built cockatoo fences around our crop, that meant saplings placed on sheer logs, one after another. However, it served the purpose for some time until we got hardwood fences up. I helped Father to fell the heavy timber and the cross cutting in many lengths to fence with, and when ready I had to carry the posts and rails and lay them on the line, miles of them, very heavy work for a frail girl. This work went on week in and week out, year by year ...

My brother made yokes for us out of limbs of the creek oak, also a slide out of slabs. We soon got our bullocks quiet and attached them to the slide with ropes. In this crude way we drew our crops home from the paddocks. Before this we had to carry it in sacks on our backs. I was mostly the packhorse ...

About this time my elder sister married, and I being the next eldest my burden was made heavier as my Mother was a very frail little woman, but she still attended to the dairy. We had a barrel churn which I helped Mother to churn to make butter. That done I had to go and help Father in the paddocks. After tea all the cleaning was done, scouring floors with stone, cleaning the butter kegs, as we were now sending our butter and produce to Broughton Creek. The steamer *Meeindery* coming once a week. The price the settlers got was 4d a pound for butter.

From now on we became more prosperous ... On one occasion there was a big sale at Kiama, a lot of mares with foals at foot advertised ... Father bought two mares with foals at foot, Father drove them over Berry Mountain to home ... and when ready we girls broke them into the side saddle for our use ... The property when the last selection was taken up was 500 acres. Father and I put up the boundary fence all round, besides numerous dividing fences, as we grew plenty of green feed for the cattle. By this time we were milking 50 cows ...

There was no use saying 'no'. I do not ever remember giving my Father and Mother a back answer. We had no hospitals, doctors, nurses or clinics in our day. No need of them ..."

Dorothy Maguire's cottage in Kangaroo Valley.

Rear view of the cottage, 1912.

A very patient grey mare, Maroon, Qld, 1907.

Rope swing at Northcliffe, W.A., 1924.

Mrs Flower, with Molly and Poppy, pose for the camera at Tilba Tilba, N.S.W.

Regardless of physical hardships, photographs of rural and outback children recall the love of fun and play, and, on occasion, dressing up for photographs.

Margaret and Bessie Organ on the goldfields at Laverton, W.A., 1918.

The Bradshaw family at Alice Springs telegraph station, N.T., 1908.

Queenie Nicholas milking, Western Australia, 1932.

The women at work milking on Christiansen's farm, Pialba, Qld, 1906.

# WOMEN'S WORK OUTSIDE THE HOME

T he role of women in many rural areas was extremely important. As well as housekeeping most shared the burden of seasonal work. On farms that grew wheat they assisted with reaping, sewing sacks and winnowing. From the earliest days they helped build the house, decorated the interior and then once the house was established, often became involved in heavier work including post and rail splitting. It is therefore surprising that women have rarely been seen as central to the physical development of colonial settlement in Australia. Men have always been identified as the pioneers and only the dynastic family lives of genteel women — wives of station owners or pastoralists — have been properly recorded in print.

In the 19th century women were seen as secondary to, and dependent on, men. As records, most women simply kept diaries or wrote letters, whereas all the written records of the farm or property were kept by the men. Thus, while the feminist pioneering histories of recent years have attempted to redress this balance, they have in a sense created feminine histories from the records of men. It is hard to alter this. However, surveying the photographs and records that remain has produced some remarkable new research on the roles of working class women, Asian women, women publicans and in particular, Aboriginal women.[1]

One study of north west Australia between 1860 and 1900 revealed that the total non-Aboriginal population, between 1881 and 1891, was 1 532. There were three major groupings — wives and daughters of European pastoralists, the servants and labourers of pastoralists and administrators, and the wives and families of merchants including the professional groups of teachers, nurses and small business managers. In the north west of Australia the growth of the pearling industry was a distinctively different economy which gave the character its fascinating history and modern racial mix. The number of women in this area grew drastically in the 1880s. Some worked in the thriving public houses, and many domestic servants married pearlers. Some Malay women came to Australia at this time working as servants and cooks, and a little known but numerically significant group of Japanese women worked as prostitutes.

Hannah (Annie) May Girdler feeding poddy calves with an old bike pump, Thargomindah, Qld. Annie had 12 children and to ensure a good supply of fresh milk, would take in poddy calves given away by passing drovers. From these calves she was able to supply the whole township with milk and cream, separating the milk and making butter by hand. She was reputed to cook the best bread in the district and fed travellers with roast or stew, cooked in the camp oven.

Not only in the north west, but throughout the cattle country of the centre and far north, by far the largest single group of women workers were Aboriginal. Most were pastoral workers although others worked as divers on pearling boats in the north west.

In the latter part of the 19th century a great many Aboriginal women travelled throughout outback areas as workers and companions.

Nineteenth century attitudes idealised pioneer women as personifying the notion of motherhood and acquiescent life partner. In fact, Australian literature in the Henry Lawson mould does not explore the complex and the non-traditional roles that women undertook during the early years of colonial settlement.

The diaries, letters and reminiscences of those whose husbands had considerable landholdings overshadowed the experiences of other less fortunate women. In such records, we are given glimpses of the shanties and shacks beyond the mainstream of life but few direct written records remain of such women. Thus a number of groups have been omitted from our historical memory — in particular Asians, poor women, single working women and of course Aboriginal women. Common variables affected them all. They experienced the same physical environment and were living in a contemporaneous pioneer frontier society. It must be remembered, whether European or Asian, the motivation of pioneers who went to new areas to set up home, farm and business was mostly personal

Transporting the milk. After rising early to milk, many women then made butter and cheese, helping to support the family through the sale or barter of dairy products.

and economic. Aboriginal women workers had little choice. Their lands were occupied and, often at the instigation of their male kin, they went to work for a new "massa" and "missus". Although many enjoyed the experience of working on cattle stations and speak today of such times with nostalgia, conditions were rough and unequal.

## DAIRYING

The labour intensive work of milking and making butter was most frequently carried out by the women. In fact it seems quite rare for the men to have worried about a supply of milk when they lived alone or with other men on their selection. Mrs Elms recalled the pioneer times in Kangaroo Valley, New South Wales:

> "Before I arrived, my brother had not troubled to milk a cow . . . his fare was salt meat, bread, rice, treacle and tea without milk, so it seemed quite a luxury to have plenty of milk, cream and butter. My first butter was churned in the milk bucket with a large homemade spoon."[2]

Butter bowl.

Oatmeal crusher.

Women feeding the calves.

As soon as the cows were obtained, most women, praising the virtues of fresh milk, took responsibility for milking and making butter and cheeses:

> "I insisted on having milking cows broken in so that we might enjoy plenty of buttermilk and cream which are luxuries that few bushmen care to be at the trouble to give themselves, and when I came up to the station I made my husband build me a nice underground dairy and undertook myself the management of it, and much enjoyed manufacturing butter and cream cheese and many delicasies [sic] which were a great treat to those whose bill of fair [sic] varied only from 'mutton, damper and tea' to 'tea, damper and mutton'."[3]

On large farms the cows were milked in stalls and many hands were needed to make butter in larger quantities. However, for a woman living on her own with many children, it was all hands to the task.

Butter churn.

## BUTTER AND CREAM

Cream separators were only introduced in the 1890s. First the milk would be put "to set" in shallow pans around the walls of the kitchen. Sometimes the cream would be skimmed off and poured into the churn which was then turned by hand. Some used a plunging device and were called "plunged churns". This was slow, repetitive physical work. The fat globules would come together and separate from the liquid buttermilk, but, in hot climates, it took a long time for the butter to congeal, so that it could be collected, mixed with salt and patted into shape with wooden butter pats. If butter was to be sold — and in many areas this was an enormous help to the housekeeping economy — a mould was used to press it into 1 pound blocks. Otherwise it was set in whatever containers were at hand.

Butter churn.

Income gained from the sale of butter financed the purchase of necessities from the local store and perhaps allowed for an occasional luxury. This was the case for the O'Reilly family who pioneered the rugged Lamington Plateau in the Macpherson Ranges, southern Queensland.[4] The O'Reillys were many kilometres from the nearest settlement. Their cream separator was bought at a high price and along with the dairy cans, had to be brought up to the farm on horseback. Cream production dominated the lives of the O'Reilly women. Cream was separated in the early hours of the morning and had to be delicately transported down the hill on horseback while it was still dark. Excessive agitation during transit would turn the cream into butter.

The task of transporting the cream often fell to Bernard's sister, Rose O'Reilly, who was an extremely competent horsewoman. She would lead the string of packhorses down the path through the rainforest to the cream stand, 12 kilometres away. From there it was picked up and taken to the factory.

## GOATS

While dairying is almost exclusively associated with cows, goats were also important milk suppliers during the early years of European settlement, and well into this century. Pictorial evidence speaks for itself — nanny goats were a much loved addition to the family pets and provided not only milk but endless fun for the children. They were also used to pull carts to town where homemade butter would be sold. Chinese market gardeners used them occasionally to cart vegetables from door to door. In far north Queensland, goats were preferred — few dairy cattle were kept in the early years of settlement. In 1892 the young schoolmaster in Laura, Cape York, remarked:

> "The goats are kept for their milk. This country is too dry for dairy cattle, except in the wet season, so we get goat's milk at six pence per quart."[5]

Goats also proved useful in keeping the grass down and if necessary could be killed and eaten.

On numerous Aboriginal missions and settlements young girls were trained to be up early and undertake the milking. Gladys Elphick lived on Point Pearce Mission in South Australia in the early 1920s. Like her mother, she rose at 4 a.m. every day and milked 23 cows by hand, repeating the process in the afternoon. She also separated the cream and cleaned the dairy.[6]

A young Aboriginal milkmaid and shepherdess. Goats were important for milk and Aboriginal women frequently undertook this work on outback stations.

Aboriginal woman shepherding goats at Bloods Creek Station, N.T.

Edith Laver feeding her pet kids in the goat pen, Alice Springs, c. 1920. (*See feature on Edith Laver, page 166.*)

# EDITH MAY LAVER

## (NEE PARKER)
## 1889–1982

Jack Laver was a World War I veteran who returned to Australia suffering from the effects of gas and shell shock. His doctors advised him to reside in the country, but while passing through Adelaide on the way to rural England, he met Edith Parker. They decided to marry and soon had their first and only child, Robert.

After working as a publican in South Australia, they took out a hotel licence in the town of Stuart in the Northern Territory. This town was renamed Alice Springs.

The Lavers' journey to Stuart was extremely difficult. The train took them as far as Oodnadatta where the line stopped. Even this was troublesome and exhausting as they encountered severe floods along the way. The journey from Adelaide to Stuart took a total of six weeks. On reaching Oodnadatta, when Edith learnt they would have to travel the remaining 630 kilometres by camel, she refused to go any further and it seemed that they would have to return to Adelaide. Eventually they were able to purchase a four-wheeled buggy that could be hitched up to horses. In this way they made the rest of the journey.

Edith was horrified when she saw their pub, the Stuart Arms. It was a dishevelled outback building that was patronised by drovers and workers who might not have seen civilisation for up to 18 months. On reaching Stuart they would "hit the liquor in a serious way".

The whole family, including young Robert, became involved in the business of the hotel. When serving the men in the bar, Edith handled them with a matronly strictness that eventually won her great respect. She would also nurse patrons through times of sickness. This was typical of Jack and Edith's attitude to the frequently lonely men who patronised their establishment.

Edith May Laver.

Jack would manage their money for them — ensuring they didn't spend six months' wages in a couple of days. He never charged them for accommodation, arguing that they spent quite enough over the bar to keep him in business.

Edith's initial despair on seeing the Stuart Arms was replaced by a desire to make the hotel more habitable. She employed a Swedish carpenter to make furniture which she stained and upholstered herself, and set about providing white sheets and pillow slips for the beds, instead of the old grey blankets. Besides working inside the hotel, Edith had many outside responsibilities, including tending the garden and looking after livestock — mainly goats and horses. The hotel garden was irrigated by water that Edith drew from a well and tipped into a wooden trough, from where it would be dispersed along a series of channels. She had spectacular success in her garden, growing all types of vegetables including beans, pumpkins and potatoes. Her record tomato weighed 1.25 kilograms.

The Lavers had several Aboriginal servants who helped in the hotel and their son Robert Laver still remembers Katie Williams, the cook, Jenny Smith, the housemaid and Angeline, the waitress. The goat shepherd was Polly. The Lavers' Aboriginal guide, George, who had led them from Oodnadatta to Stuart, remained in their employ until they left the town.

At this time Stuart had 27 European settlers. Besides Edith, there were only seven other white women in the vicinity. For this reason, it was a tight-knit community and social occasions, picnics and race days played an important part in the women's lives.

Edith Laver out riding near Stuart (later named Alice Springs).

Edith Laver, her son Bob Laver seated on a horse, and Aboriginal guides on the journey to Stuart.

Edith Laver behind the bar at the Stuart Arms Hotel.

Mrs Laver photographed walking at Heavitree Gap towards the Police Station residence.

Riding on the haycart after harvest, Western Australia, 1923.

## WHEAT FARMING

In the mid-1840s almost all farm work was done by hand. The whole family shared the work of ploughing, broadcasting the seed and harvesting. Wheat was cut with a sickle, bound, stooked, thrown onto a dray and carted and thrown onto the stack. A threshing machine then separated the grain from the stalks and young girls often helped in this activity.

> "Uncle and my sisters and myself in turn thrashed. Lucy goes first, then Bessie has a little turn before dinner, and again for a short time after, then R.A. and I finish. It requires some activity and is capital exercise, we leave the barn with glowing cheeks. Uncle has a nice easy job, he stands in front of the machine, and with a pointed stick draws the straw away after it is thrashed into a heap. Tom takes it from this heap with a fork ... and hurls it out at the barn door for the benefit of the pigs."[7]

In South Australia the story of the development of wheat is a microcosm of its growing importance over succeeding years to the colony as a whole.

South Australian farmers preferred to grow wheat as it was a certain crop whereas wool was a gamble with higher rewards. In 1889, Anthony Trollope remarked:

> "South Australian farmers simply live comfortably and die in obscurity by growing wheat; but South Australian squatters make splendid fortunes or are ruined magnificently by growing wool."[8]

Women and children assist the men in the wheat harvest, at "Rosedale", Narrogin, W.A., 1914.

The harvest at Morawa, W.A., 1914.

However, yields soon subsided as problems arose. Owing to the incidence of red dust in wheat two thirds of farms were not large enough to produce an adequate return although wheat proceeds increased enormously after the discovery of gold in Victoria and the increased market for flour on the goldfields.

In 1886 the South Australian Government helped with a system of scrub leases in the mallee, a despised area where the mallee stems had to be chopped, the ground opened, and the spiked log dragged over the surface. However, determined farmers mastered this. R. B. Smith of Kalkabury on the York Peninsula invented the unique stump jump plough in 1876 and from this time the obstacles to farming the mallee lands were reduced. A scramble for land followed.

Vast areas were "grubbed" — a term which describes the uprooting of stumps. Horsepower was quickly replaced by tractors and mallee farmers soon transferred their loyalty. The wide uses to which the kerosene tin and cases were put in these areas is related to the fact that the first tractors were kerosene fueled.

At harvest time women often brought morning tea to the men.

Armidale, N.S.W.

Drouin, Vic.

Women's Land Army workers. During wartime, women were called on to work on the farms in place of men.

Clara McNabb ploughing the wheat field in the Victorian mallee district, 1920s. (*See feature on Clara McNabb, page 102.*)

A sturdy, handmade wooden wheelbarrow still in use at Jamberoo, N.S.W.

Yields of wheat varied tremendously but women were always required to assist in various tasks whether starting the tractor in the morning with hot water from the stove, sewing the bags as they were lined up in the open, or clearing sticks and burning them before planting. Many old photographs show women and children helping to stook the wheat.

In many country industries, additional labour was often required on the farm to clear the land or harvest and at this time women's work increased greatly. There was extra cooking and sometimes a great deal of extra washing to be done — of dishes and clothes. Rural "industrial relations" decreed that working men had to be happy with their food and conditions. The role of many women in providing this was a definite and valuable contribution to the farm economy.

Young girls or farmers' daughters were employed pulling up "drake" or "darnel", a weed that grew amongst the crop. The younger children also had to remain constantly on guard watching for cockatoos and chasing them off the wheat. Mrs J. Fairfax Conigrave describes working in the wheat paddocks as a young child:

> "One day Papa discovered a certain obnoxious weed had come up with the wheat ('drake' it was called), and it would never do to let it ripen, as it would injure the sale of the crop for seed wheat, and, as good wheat was scarce, it must be got rid of; so what better 'recreation for the children' could be devised than putting them to clear it by pulling up each separate plant? . . . My two brothers, Jane, and myself, were taken to the paddock, and shown our work.
>
> I know *we* did not regard it as recreation, by any means, but there was no help for it — the 70 acre paddock had to be cleared of it. We each took our portion of the field, and began the eradicating business.
>
> How I hated to see that plant shining there in the sun, that one could not possibly mistake it, although I think occasionally we left a plant here and there."[9]

The harvest was often in the nature of a family outing, although a very hardworking one. Sometimes the community would rally and groups of workers would move from one paddock to another helping with the harvest. Many remember its pleasures. There would be picnics in the fields and although the work was hard it was often an enjoyable social event.

> "Then for me came the only exciting part of wheat-loading. The horse now attached to the team, I was free to scramble up on the load. I can still smell the fragrance of the new jute wheat bags and feel that creak and crunch of the weight beneath me as the horses strained to shift the heavy load. The hot sun drew sweetness from the crushed stubble, and a lark would whir away into the air, rising higher and higher, until it melted into the cloudless sky, leaving behind its wild sweet trilling.
>
> My father would drive the load back to our house where my mother waited at the gate with a box of cut lunch and bottled tea. I would jump down from the wagon and the wheat would be on its way to the Yongala railway station nine miles away. In the later afternoon we would hear the rumble of the empty wagon returning, carried briskly along by the horses eager for home and food."[10]

## ITINERANT WORK

Due to Australia's diverse geographical areas and extremes in climate, the new settlers had to adjust their agriculture and develop many different crops. In Tasmania's cold climate hops were easily grown. As early as 1820, two breweries had commenced and by 1829 there were five in Hobart alone. Hops cultivation was shortly followed by other cold climate berry fruits and, later, apples.

Women pickers were important in the hops industry and in South Australia early photographs of the beginnings of the wine industry show a large number of women and children harvesting the grapes.

Seasonal work, particularly picking — apples, oranges, bananas or cotton — has remained an important survival component both for white and Aboriginal itinerant rural workers. Many of these groups have included large numbers of women. These numbers grew during the 1939–45 war when women rallied to the call of the "Women's Land Army" and went in place of men to country areas to labour on farms, and pick fruit.

Women picking hops in Tasmania, early 20th century.

Apple picking in Tasmania, 1912. Seasonal picking remains important work for large numbers of itinerant rural workers. Many of these groups have included large numbers of women.

## SHEARING AND SHEEP

There is less evidence of the involvement of women in the wool industry than in wheat and cattle; however, there are exceptions to the rule that the shearing shed was universally the male dominated bastion of mateship and hard work.

German women were reported as being excellent shearers in several areas of South Australia. Jane Isabella Watts speaks of a comfortable sheep station at the source of the Torrens, about 30 kilometres from Adelaide. The scenery was parklike with walks and rides reminiscent to her of the "Old Country". When the shearing came on she often strolled down to the woolsheds to watch the sheep being washed and shorn.

> "The latter process was principally performed by German women who seemed to do it quite as expertly as the men, and were not so rough in handling the shears, thereby causing less pain to the poor patient animal who are often terribly cut about by 'green hands', and must suffer acutely in consequence."[11]

Mary Ann Eade in the woolshed at "Lilydale", Booligal, N.S.W., at the turn of the century.

Minnie Bilton feeding her pet lambs on the farm in Maryborough, Vic., 1914. (*See feature on Bette Bilton, page 147.*)

Poorer women were commonly employed as shepherds. In many areas, children were also engaged to watch sheep and goats. This task also fell to Aboriginal women who were often employed in a group on sheep stations picking out the burrs or generally cleaning and sorting fleeces. Aboriginal women preferred to work together in groups. The traditional working practice of Aboriginal women was to gather food in groups, and as well it afforded them some protection — they could undertake the work well apart from the shearers.

Dray with wool bales, Woolpack Inn Museum, Holbrook, N.S.W.

The Bohning family, Helen Springs station, N.T., 1925. The Bohning girls were known as "the petticoat drovers".

Leith Eggins camp drafting at Theodore, Qld.

## WORKING "IN THE CATTLE"

In Australia's outback pioneering history some women have achieved fame —
although often it is their nickname which survives rather than memories of
their great deeds. Elsie Bohning, who wrote under the pseudonym "The Little
Bush Maid", was known as a "petticoat drover" along with her sister and her
mother, Esther Bohning.

Esther and John Bohning worked Helen Springs Station, 160 kilometres
north of Tennant Creek. All the family including Esther, and her two daughters and sons, were fully active partners in the property. They rode, mustered
and branded stock and went on cattle drives. At times they had to manage the
station on their own. Elsie went on her first drove at the age of 11 and eulogised
it in the following lines:

> *I am travelling down the OT line and I'm a drover's hand,*
> *I am handy making Johnny cakes — I am handy with the pan.*
> *And I can bend a mob of steers*
> *Did you hear my stockwhip crack?*
> *No, stockwhips are forbidden with fat cattle on the track.*
> *Now all you jolly rovers from hut and camp and town,*
> *Come drink the health of the drover, the king of the overland.*[12]

There were many women who rode behind the cattle across two states. They
were wives and daughters of drovers, camp cooks, and a few were boss drovers
of some repute. May Steele was a famous boss drover of Queensland and the
Northern Territory. During the 1939–45 war, she and her husband Jack battled
across with more than a 1 000 head of bullocks. They doubled jobs in daylight
hours and rationed their sleep at night. Such trips were epics of endurance. A
small reserved woman, in a prim Victorian shirt, her appearance belies the
gritty strength that was her nature.[13]

Another woman drover to achieve renown in the late 1940s was Edna
Zigenbine, who absorbed the skill and techniques of the well-known Queensland and Territory drover, Harry Zigenbine. She spent much of her childhood
on the road with cattle and although she had no formal education, learnt to
master horses and cattle.

She was renowned as a reliable drover with bullocks but had a skill with cows
and calves which surpassed any man.

> "She'd mother them up and nurse them along; must have been the female instinct
> to care for the young. Give Edna a mob of cows and calves; there'd be calves born
> on the road, and Edna would deliver more cattle than she started out with."[14]

179

# GLADYS BAUER

## b. 1916
## DROVER'S COOK

*Twenty Weeks from the Territory to Walgett, across three states.*

"In the year 1942 my eldest son Alan had his 14th birthday. He wanted to leave school and go on the road droving with his father. I thought about it for some time. We had four other children, Beryl 12, Colleen 10, Ray 8, Lee 6 and because my husband was away for months at a time Alan and I decided our life wasn't much the way it was. No electricity in our old house only kerosene lamps and board floor. Very little money most of the time — so cold in winter. As I was on my own with the children most of the year I began to wonder how I would get on without Alan as he was a great help. So we talked it over and discovered if I went cooking on a droving trip and he went as a ringer we would earn £10 each a week. We talked about a little Austin car we could buy when we came back, line and seal our old home and best of all, Electricity. So when Henry came home we had it all planned. I could not take the children on the road as I would have five men to cook for so my sister who lived in Tambo and had three children of her own said she would board Ray and the two girls and I would have to take Lee with me. He had a

mind of his own and I knew he would not stop, so when the next trip came up we had our plans ready. Henry had a new Austin Truck, and I had to learn to drive it and get a licence. I turned out to be a good truck driver on all kinds of bush roads by the time the first trip was over. So all we had to do now was pack enough gear for 3 or 4 months and get the kids settled in Tambo. Henry got his men together, Stan Fletcher as horse-tailer, Ronnie Wade as ringer, and Alan and Red Hannan, about Alan's age also, ringers and me as cook. They trucked the horses at Winton and got to Mt Isa. Stan went with them on the train and we went by lorry to Mt Isa and took delivery of 1 350 head of bullocks at a place called Warrany Station ... This was where I really found out what I had to do to earn that £10. A drover's cook had to rise at 3 a.m. and make breakfast for five men, so they would be ready when the horse tailer came with the horses. He had to rise at 3 a.m. I had got a supply of bread at Mt Isa so didn't have to make bread for a few days. We only had potatoes, pumpkin, onions, so it had to be a stew, curry or mince

Overnight camp in 1905. The Bradshaw family with others at Owen Springs, N.T. No photographs survive of Gladys Bauer on her journey, yet life for women on the track changed little in the intervening years between this photograph and her journey in 1942.

for breakfast, cooked in a big camp oven. We always had plenty of meat, mostly corned. We had no way of keeping it fresh and you had to soak it for hours before you cooked it or it was too salty.

The men left the next morning with the cattle and I had to pack up the lorry and go to the next camp. Henry would tell me where to go — about 9 miles sometimes. If I didn't pick the right place, I heard about it when Henry got there late in the afternoon. Sometimes I had to pack up again and shift to suit the Boss. As we went from camp to camp I found out there was one important thing to remember on the road and that was a good camp for the cattle and to fill the water tank on the lorry if we passed a watering place. One of the boys would always help fill the tank as you had to fill it with a bucket and it was hard work and so also was my washing.

When the ringers wanted clean clothes they carried them on their saddles and on dinner camp would have a swim change clothes and wash the dirty ones and hang them on a bush to dry. I carried a tub and when I did the washing at a waterhole, would put it on a drum to wash and I would carry the clothes in a bucket to the camp and put a rope from tree to tree to hang the clothes on. If there were no trees, I would hang a rope from the truck onto a peg hammered into the ground. I always had a bath when I got to the camp. No men about, I couldn't go for a swim as I never learnt to swim.

From Warrany Station we went to Lake Nash Dip travelling along the border fence, ninety miles. The Inspector was there and the men had to dip the cattle. So we had a day there and that's where I made my first lot of potato yeast and made a batch of bread in a big camp oven. I didn't do so well for a few batches. The coals were either too hot or too cold but when you depend on bread so much I soon got used to it . . . when you tapped it, and it had a hollow sound you knew you had good bread. Bun loaf is bread dough with sugar and sultanas added.

Stan, the horse-tailer, was supposed to get wood for me each day but most times Lee and I had to get it ourselves. The next town we passed was Urandangel. . .

Stocked up on more spuds and pumpkin there, then travelled slowly on to Dajarra where we struck 8 inches of rain. That's where I learned to swear like the ringers. Although we had a tarpaulin over the lorry all the time I had to climb up the back of it whenever I wanted anything. Henry had a ladder made for me to climb up on but it was still hard work. By this time I was fed up with camp ovens and boiling salt meat. I soon learnt to make a good bun loaf and a brownie in the camp oven by the time we passed Dutchess then Bulia 133 miles from Dajarra. I was getting used to packing and unpacking the lorry every day. It was only the thoughts of improving our lives a bit that kept me going. Although Henry and I were together we didn't see much of each other. He left the camp at daylight with the cattle and got back to the camp about dark most nights when the cattle were put on camp. He would watch them until the men would have their supper then Alan or Red would go out and do 2 hours watch each, then Stan and Wadey would do their turn and Henry always did the last watch and would wake me at 3 o'clock to cook breakfast and the horse-tailer to get the horses and they would be gone again by daylight. Same old thing day after day, but we were steadily getting there . . .

I was always worried at night time, expecting the cattle to rush. They did one night in a terrible storm, thunder and lightning was terrible, the night was so black and all I could see was a big black mass moving around restless, and I was scared as the two boys were on watch and all of a sudden the cattle rushed. A terrible noise and I would hear Alan calling to Red. He had got thrown from his horse and I couldn't see either of them until they came into camp. Alan wasn't hurt but the cattle were all gone. It was the worst night we had in 20 weeks on the road. It took all the men next day to get them together again. Lee . . . was becoming a good woodchopper. By this time he had a tommy axe of his own and walked around all day chopping anything he could find . . .

From there we were on our way to New South Wales. Walgett was our destination. We travelled through Isisford to Blackall, our home town . . . we would see Ray and the girls as we passed through and as school holidays were coming up we planned to take them with us. I didn't know how I was going to manage with four kids on the road but found they were no trouble at all. Ray was a good horseman and went with his father each day and Henry was pleased to have his two sons with him as Alan was an old hand at droving by this time and the girls helped me do jobs about the camp . . .

The men took lunches every day which meant I had to have meat and bread and brownies every day ready for the next day. So we next passed Bollon then Hebel another 97 mile. It was only a post office there and when I walked into it the first thing I saw was a photo of a Blackall boy, Roy Dunn, riding a billy goat over a jump, 3 feet 6 inches high, a record. Turned out his aunty was working the post office there. All getting very tired now except the kids who were having a great time riding ponies and finding plenty to do round the bush. I was back cursing bread and camp ovens again, but our goal was getting close now. I could see myself with a new car and planning what we would do to our old house when we got back home.

At long last we arrived in Walgett 20 weeks of weary travelling and just in time as the rain was coming, rivers running. We stayed there a few days while the men were trucking the cattle and having a look at the town. Then we headed for home . . . and I have never touched a camp oven since. But we got our new car and a nice house and best of all, Electricity."

## ABORIGINAL WOMEN

Aboriginal women were widely employed on the expanding cattle stations in the remote outback of the north of Australia, both within the home and beyond. They worked at a range of jobs far wider than might normally be expected of women. Many worked in various types of stock management, mustering, tailing cattle, procuring killers for homestead meals and riding beside men as drovers.

Aboriginal women were considered as more malleable and pliable than men. In order to disguise the extensive employment of Aboriginal women, many station owners and drovers issued men's work clothing so that the term "drover's boys" became widespread. The use of men's clothing was an attempt to give the team respectability. By 1911, a new ordinance to the Aboriginals Act made it an offence for an Aboriginal woman to be in "male attire and in the company of any male person other than an Aboriginal or half-caste", a rule which was impossible to enforce and was largely ignored.

The importance of Aboriginal women in the development of the cattle industry has been largely underestimated, although men such as Bill Harney who was married to an Aboriginal woman, used female stock workers on Seven Emus Station and commended his own companion for her tracking skills particularly in searching for stray cattle.

Aboriginal women shared the workload equally including night watches and were highly valued as they were adept at catching game and therefore providing meat for the camp oven. Many were employed as camp cooks. While looked down on by the white outback fraternity, the lengthy association between Aboriginal women and white men in the cattle industry has markedly affected the history of the Northern Territory, giving rise to its particular and unique culture.

On most cattle stations, the Aborigines whose tribal lands had been usurped settled in camps somewhat detached from the main homestead and close to an appropriate water supply. From time to time these groups would move according to the seasons as was the traditional behaviour pattern. It was this practice and the associated need for young men to absent themselves to undergo initiations which gave rise to the derogatory term "going walkabout". In later decades this "habit" came to describe what white employers saw as a footloose quality in Aboriginal employees which mitigated against their receiving any responsibilities in the workforce (or equal pay).

The tasks which Aboriginal women undertook in the formation and settlement of Australia were many and diverse. They worked as shepherds for goats, sheep and mules and this included feeding, milking and transporting them to distant places or from waterhole to waterhole. They were often responsible for the messy side of housekeeping — slaughtering small animals like chickens or

Nellie Flynn and Tom, a ganger on the railway, Northern Territory.

The Aboriginal community at Wattie Creek, N.T., 1970. The lives of women — the cooking, water carting and station work — changed little over decades in many outback areas.

goats and butchering them for the kitchen. They helped in the construction of homes by stripping bark or sinking posts, they gathered ant beds for use as flooring. Very often women worked as a group as it is the traditional custom even when food gathering, and it is not surprising that the white children of the household invariably enjoyed their early experiences if they had Aboriginal nannies or childminders. To judge from the numerous photographs that survive in archival collections Aboriginal women, rather than white women, were the female founders of contemporary Northern Territory society — and their role is vastly underestimated. The tasks were so numerous that they entail all aspects of life which required knowledge of the environment. They were valued as workers because of their strength and resilience, as well as knowledge of animal habits and waterholes. Their technical skills such as the ability to dig yams and roots or survive in remote places or even make a good string or rope from bush bark were valuable. Aboriginal women were invariably the woodchoppers for the fuel stove which cooked the meals not only for the household but also for the station workers.

Aboriginal women usually gave up droving when they had their first child. It was a fact of life that their babies could not be transported on the horses on long rides. Amy Laurie was born in about 1913. Her parents were Aboriginal but she was brought up by a white drover. As a teenager she worked in general stockwork and later married a stockman.

> "We worked the bullocks the same as the boys . . . All the women from every station went droving. Women like it, liked to be alone, droving . . . but as drovers changed the horses every day it was too dangerous to carry a child in the saddle. 'It might be a wild horse or a quiet horse, you don't know.' "[15]

The relationship between Aboriginal women and white women in the homesteads were varied and mixed. In the writings of the period, particularly Mrs Aeneas Gunn's *We of the Never Never* and of the journalist, Ernestine Hill, descriptions of the domestic goings-on reveal attitudes of the white women as bemused tolerance.

Although Mrs Aeneas Gunn spoke of the incongruous goings-on in the kitchen as "a perpetual circus and variety show on the premises", on the Aboriginal side the memories are different. Some were taken from the camps as children and subsequently educated and reared in the white homestead. Winnie Chapman worked in the 1920s as a domestic servant on one of the Durack properties. It was a process of being "reared up". She was shown everything from washing up to laying the table. On another property an Aboriginal woman might be taught to sew, embroider, knit and generally make herself useful in the evenings as well as the days. These skills, of course, stood them in good stead later, repairing clothes for their own families. The terminology of the day is typically racist. Teaching Aboriginal women domestic work was

Aboriginal women at the Alice Springs telegraph station, photographed between 1921 and 1926. The most common tasks undertaken by women, apart from domestic work, were carting water and carrying firewood.

Amelia Kunoth with the young Edna Bradshaw, Alice Springs telegraph station, 1906.

Runge, Tryff and the Bradshaw children at Alice Springs telegraph station, 1906. The Bradshaws were the first family to live at the telegraph station.

Dolly with Donnell Bradshaw, 1901.

often referred to as "breaking in", and Aboriginal women were universally known as "gins" or "lubras".

Young Aboriginal girls, sometimes under 10 years of age, would be sent by their mothers or by older men to work in the homestead. Initially they might simply cart wood, clean away rubbish or weed the gardens. Later they would be taught to wash clothes and iron, although this was fraught with danger, with the possibility of scorching the delicate white clothing of the homestead. A more senior position was that of cook or breadmaker. The use of Aboriginal women as house cleaners was universal. Tasks included sweeping or mopping the verandah, raking around the homestead or dampening the ground to keep dust down.

Aboriginal women also provided company for white women whose husbands were away for protracted periods of time. In such situations friendships grew. The relations between Aboriginal women and the white employers should therefore not be dismissed lightly, as being so unequal as not to have fundamental human bonds. Many women today recall the closeness of the friendships which developed and the affection held by older Aboriginal women for the mistresses in later life and vice versa.[16]

The skills and knowledge of older Aboriginal women were a great asset to the station. Some such natural leaders, sometimes wives of the most influential men, could easily rouse their relatives to work harder and keep to timetables if they so desired.

Aboriginal women were essential and gifted midwives. They delivered babies and nursed white women on many stations, using their knowledge of manipulation, massage, herbal medicine and traditional hygiene. There were remedies for lack of milk, and the use of kino and eucalyptus oil as antiseptic fumigants was widespread. It was also common for Aboriginal women to act as wetnurse for babies when the mother was ill. Sometimes this was clandestine as many households felt a certain degree of distaste for this activity, although it is the Aboriginal women's natural way of babysitting.

A rare photograph of the Piccoli family with their extensive racks of silkworms, from which the women extracted silk. They were members of a little-known, small Italian community which settled at Woodburn, N.S.W., in the late 19th century. The area was known as "New Italy".

# OUTSIDERS

mmigrant groups outside the Anglo-Celtic mainstream arrived in the early years of European settlement in Australia. Most prominent were the German communities of South Australia and the Chinese, "Afghan" and Indian merchants and camel drovers who came to forge communication and supply links throughout the interior. In Queensland a significant South Sea Island, Melanesian, or "Kanak", community remained after being forcibly imported as labour to establish the sugar industry, and in South Australia, Cornish miners formed a separate, small group. Other smaller communities came and then dissipated.

In custom, tradition, language, housing and often dress, the women of each of these groups developed distinctive approaches to their new land. Each was perceived, in varying degrees, to be "different", or "outside" the norm. As a consequence, the "outsiders" retained a separateness and distinctiveness designed to protect the group and give it cohesiveness.

Many Afghans, Chinese and Islanders sought company and refuge with Aborigines, who were, from the beginning, also considered "outsiders" in their own land.

## CORNISH WOMEN IN SOUTH AUSTRALIA

In the 1860s large numbers of Cornish immigrants appeared in the new colonies congregating in South Australia. Most were miners who settled in the towns of Burra and Moonta where copper had been discovered. The experience of Cornish women in Australia was certainly pioneering. The Burra area was divided into five towns in which villages of Cornish design sprang up. Most were small cottages with a low, squat appearance and some underground sections.

A number of miners built dugouts in the bed of the Burra Creek, the dry channel forming an easy road to work instead of trekking through the mallee and the scrub. One observer described them as "rather like rabbit holes with only 1 or 2 feet between each house and the dividing wall, usually just a mud bank. Some had only one room but others had three or four . . . the chimneys were something of a hazard for pedestrians who tripped over them, while goats often fell in".[1] The dugouts had white-washed walls, single verandahs and were relatively cool in summer although they only had holes for doors and windows.

A comfortable Cornish cottage in Moonta, S.A., built in 1870 by John Wood.

By 1851 approximately 2 600 people were living in about 600 dugouts; the remains of some are preserved today.

The conditions at Moonta were better. There, comfortable cottages of stone and clay were built with timber roofs and fittings. Castor oil bottles with the bottoms cut off were sometimes inserted in the walls as ventilators.

Cornish women lived much as they had in Cornwall and maintained all domestic customs including making rag rugs to cover the floor. Like most pioneer women they had their babies at home and sewed their families' clothes by candlelight. They baked Cornish pasties for their husbands to take to work and packed them with a piece of Cornish seed cake in white crib bags tied at the top with tape. Christmas was celebrated in the Cornish way. It began with Carols by Candlelight, representing the candles from miners' hats. Hundreds of worshippers would set out early in the morning to reach the churches in time for the early morning service. The chapels were decorated with green branches and traditional Cornish music would be played on flutes, ophicleides, serpents and bassoons. After church a parade would pass through town singing with more joining along the way.[2]

Cornish families outside a miner's cottage at Yelta, S.A., 1902.

Young woman photographed amongst the banana trees at Farnborough, Qld, c. 1895.

## MELANESIAN WOMEN OF THE CANE FIELDS

Queensland's tropical coast provided opportunities for early settlers to develop new crops. From 1860 the Civil War in the United States of America interrupted cotton production. World prices soared and Queensland farmers began to grow cotton. There was not an adequate labour force in Queensland to work cotton farms. As a result, a landowner named Robert Town decided to import South Sea Islanders, "Kanaks", or Melanesians, as labourers to grow his cotton and the sugar farmers followed his lead.

Sugar quickly spread from Brisbane north to Maryborough and Mackay. The Islander workers found the northern tropical areas easier to deal with. Although the term "Kanak" is not widely used by the descendants of these Islanders today in Australia, it is still widely used by the Melanesian people of the Pacific.

The iniquitous trade in Island labour has been likened to the historic slave trade of the American deep south. Even the term "plantation" was adopted here.

A large group of women labourers with their "overseer" on the canefields at Cairns, Qld, 1890.

Islander women and men walking behind the plough to plant sugarcane by hand. The photograph, taken at Bingera, Qld, c. 1897, shows the backbreaking work required.

Although, on their arrival at a Queensland port, the Islanders had the legal right to decline to complete their labour agreements and to return to their home islands, few knew of this condition and had little recourse but to serve out their terms.

The Islanders lived permanently on the plantations. One proud planter remarked:

> "Not only do they do their work well, but they are contented. I do not put them on rations; they get all they require of beef, sweet potatoes, yams, corn meal, green corn, arrowroot, sugar, molasses, milk and one plug of tobacco per week. Tea they do not care about; when they want tea they are not afraid to ask for it."[3]

Small Islander "villages" on stilts with large components of thatch grew up. Using their island agricultural techniques, the workers grew whatever crops they could to supply their food needs.

The number of women who came with the men was quite disproportionate. In 1888 in the Bundaberg district there were 2 043 Islander men employed in sugar plantations, and 134 Islander women. Yet, in comparison to the number of white women employed in the sugar farms, they were by far the majority. Reports of the planters show lack of understanding of the social ties that bound the women to the men they accompanied:

> "Late in 1880 two females arrived, one being married. Her husband was drafted to Inverness but she was sent to Mielere, three miles to the west. 'It was proposed to the lady that she should make her choice of one of the boys on Mielere plantation . . .' but she, refusing such a proposal, 'ran away and, like a kangaroo, made tracks for Inverness and threw herself into the arms of her delighted husband who clasped his faithful wife to his manly bosom'. It was not the end of the story; the following Sunday, Angus Bell found a warlike group had arrived from Mielere intending to reclaim the runaway. They were quickly beaten off."[4]

From 1884, legislation restricted the employment of Islanders. Although there was great public outrage, many Queensland towns had developed major sugar industries as a result of Town's initial experiment. Many Islanders returned home, assisted by the government. Many more remained, however, and continued a distinctive cultural life in Australia, marked by great skill in fruit growing and vegetable production. The distinctive cultural and social customs of Islander women, including coconut palm weaving, gift-giving and extensive hospitality, continues to the present day.

The communities of Islanders who lived on sugar or banana plantations built their own small villages and many had self-sufficient gardens of fruit or vegetables.

Islander or "Kanak" women and children at Farnborough, Qld, c. 1895.

Children of the Hambledon sugar plantation, photographed with the Islander staff, c. 1891.

## GERMAN WOMEN SETTLERS

German communities began coming to Australia in the late 1830s after George Fyfe Angus managed to convince Pastor Kavel and his flock of Lutherans to leave the religious persecution in Germany and emigrate to Australia. The first of the ships bringing them, the *Prince George*, set forth from Hamburg and arrived in South Australia in November 1838. The second ship, the *Zebra*, arrived in December 1838, under the command of Dirk Meinertz Hahn. Settlers from the earlier ship had begun to take up land owned by Angus on the River Torrens at Klemzig, which was named after a village which many had left behind in Germany. Captain Hahn was perturbed to hear on arrival that the land was not very productive and encouraged his passengers to take up land in the Mount Barker district. They moved to a new village there which they named Hahndorf in honour of the captain.

In the early days German settlers faced hunger and considerable hardship. Many early houses were built with a mixture of straw and mud and while the architecture was clearly derived from traditional European practice the buildings varied greatly. Slab-sided, thatch-roofed stores, mud and stone barns, timber houses with panels infilled with wattle and daub as well as brick houses were all built by German settlers. The original buildings were single-room cottages. As communities grew more prosperous, more sophisticated houses were built with two or more rooms as well as kitchen parlours. Essentially, the houses were built in farm villages.

German pioneering women have a reputation as being extraordinarily hard workers. They had a tradition of partnership within the home; their domestic role was not as clearly circumscribed as was the English-Irish tradition under the Victorian ideal. In addition, women of the German hamlets had the advantage of social contact with each other — which must not be underestimated and, with this social safety net, the hard physical rigours of working in all roles of farming life was more easily accepted.

By the 1890s some German women had become famous orchardists. In 1910 one indomitable character, Mrs Hauber, together with her sons and daughters, built a new six-roomed stone house in the area of Wirrabara. This was a famous fruit growing area by this time and Mr Hauber took charge of the vegetable round while his family managed the garden. The elder children helped their mother to quarry the stone from the hillside, mix the mortar and build the walls.[5]

German women pioneer settlers were praised as excellent shearers, fruit pickers, builders and gardeners. The legacy of their domestic culture and distinctive German food traditions remain a facet of many Australian families. The story of Ottilie Johannsen is interesting for the innovative and resilient way in which she coped with isolation and lack of supplies. The wife of an early stonemason, she first lived at Hermannsburg Mission. The food she prepared for her family was adapted from German tradition. In her home cooking she made the most of available spices but augmented them with Aboriginal bush food. Because of her connection with the German settlers of the Barossa Valley she was able to send for bulk food supplies that other pioneering women would not have thought of, or probably wanted. She sent for large supplies of dried fruit for example, as well as the usual flour, tea and sugar. Adept at gardening, she collected seeds and soon grew date palms. The palms which still survive at Hermannsburg were grown from the seeds from the dates sold by Afghan hawkers to the German missionaries.

During World War II hundreds of German place names were wiped from the map of Australia and many law-abiding people were interned. The German pioneering influence and the distinctive domestic culture of German women has therefore been hidden in many areas of the country.

Ottilie Johannsen (at left) with the Aboriginal child she fostered for a year and then returned to the family, c. 1909. Ottilie, the wife of a German stonemason was a pioneer of the mission at Hermannsburg and later of Deep Well, N.T. (*See feature on Ottilie Johannsen, page 202*).

# MARIE OTTILIE JOHANNSEN

## (NEE HOFFMAN)
## 1881–1959

Marie Ottilie Hoffman was the fifth child and only daughter of Carl Johann Hoffman and Marie Dorothea Guntea, a young German couple who arrived in South Australia in 1878 and settled in the Barossa Valley. When Ottilie (Tilly) was about nine, she helped the family by shepherding neighbours' cows up and down the creek to earn a little extra money. As a teenager she walked many kilometres into Angaston and worked at a cannery to earn money for dressmaking lessons. This was to be very useful in her later pioneering life in Central Australia.

In 1905, at the age of 23, Ottilie Hoffman married a young Dane, Gerhardt Andreas Johannsen, a professional stonemason and builder. His craft had been put to good use in the Barossa Valley where he built the Stockwell Church in 1904, and other small cottages.

In 1909, Gerhardt took up a position at Hermannsburg, the German Aboriginal Mission settlement in Central Australia. The family travelled by train to the railhead at Oodnadatta and thence overland by horse and buggy mail coach. The track from Oodnadatta to Hermannsburg followed well-known waterholes until it reached the dry bed of the Finke River. Along the river the young family would stop occasionally for water at various soaks (shallow wells dug into the dry sand lined with pieces of split timber to keep the sand from falling into the water). In Ottilie's subsequent life in Central Australia, she was often thrown on her own resources as her husband was away from home for lengthy periods on government contracts, geological surveys and mining exploration. At times he also acted as guide to explorers, anthropologists and travellers, including H. Basedow, Sir Baldwin Spencer and the Duttons.

The family first lived at Hermannsburg, then moved to Deep Well, and later to Alice Springs. At Hermannsburg, Gerhardt worked with the Aboriginal men to build the now historic stone houses as well as the cattleyards and to sink wells and carry out general station work. Ottilie taught Aboriginal women how to "keep house", adding the skills of sewing, embroidery and crochet.

Ottilie Johannsen and her daughter Elsa on a camel.

Deep Well station, 80 kilometres south of Alice Springs.

Ottilie and Elsa Johannsen in 1910.

In 1911 Gerhardt obtained a government contract to water travelling stock at Deep Well, 80 kilometres south of Alice Springs. The well was on 259 hectares of land, and a short time later he took over the lease of crown land which surrounded the well. Deep Well provided water for cattle being driven from the Top End to the Oodnadatta railhead. It also provided water for Afghan camel trains which carried all the supplies from Oodnadatta north to the settlements every two to six months.

The first home occupied by Ottilie, Gerhardt and their baby daughter was three separate log cabins with thatched roofs that had been built by the previous family. Walls were lined with newspaper, and flat flagstones formed the floors. The cracks between them were filled with fat and sifted ashes. At night, they used tallow candles made with a cloth wick set in a tin of sand and topped with fat. Kerosene lanterns were only for special occasions or for the table.

At Deep Well Gerhardt built a stone house for the family and they kept goats which were used as the main meat and were milked and shepherded by

an Aboriginal family. Gerhardt was absent frequently. He built the stone police station at Altunga Goldfields in 1912 and also at Alice Well.

The family was proud of their new four-roomed stone house at Deep Well. The ceilings were slabs of split desert oak impervious to white ants and trimmed with an adze. The floors were flat stones and the doors were hand-sawn kurrajong, a soft desert timber. The extensive verandahs were used as storerooms and fly-wired sleepouts.

Ottilie had two more children — Gertrude in 1912 and Kurt in 1915. Both were delivered by their father.

Some of the stories the family recollects of their mother's life reveal the danger and isolation in which she found herself and her resourcefulness in all circumstances. On one such occasion she went to bring in the cows which were kept for milk. They had strayed into the sandhills because there were no fences, and sometimes they went long distances, especially after rain. She went out in the evening but did not return. Her three young children were becoming upset. Gerhardt had a premonition that something was wrong and came

Gerhardt and Ottilie Johannsen with three of their children outside their home at Deep Well. The two youngest in this photograph were delivered by their father.

204

home. It was too late by then to follow tracks. The family waited all night. Ottilie had been found by Aboriginal stockmen and was brought back next morning on horseback.

On another occasion when quite alone, Ottilie found an Afghan camel driver, who had broken into the storeroom, standing in her house in the middle of the night. She always kept a rifle or small bore shotgun handy to shoot snakes that came in from the spinifex. They would enter the house through mouseholes and hide behind the homemade kerosene tin cupboards. According to her daughter, "Mother was a good shot, even when it was difficult to see by a lantern's light".

In 1923–24 the family was asked to take over management of the Mission Station at Hermannsburg, as Pastor Carl Strehlow had passed away. Their daughter Mona was born at Hermannsburg in 1923. Gerhardt began a tannery at the Mission and established a vegetable garden while Ottilie resumed her teaching and introduced embroidery and crochet to the women, now assisted by her daughter, Elsa. As well, it was necessary to supervise Trudy and Kurt's daily correspondence lessons.

On their return to Deep Well, Ottilie had two more children, Randall and Myrtle, both of whom were delivered again by her husband. During the early stages of labour Gerhardt took the other children to a gully in the hills a few kilometres from home for a picnic where they could play in the sandy waterholes. Then, leaving the older children in charge, he went back to deliver the baby.

By 1928, Deep Well had become badly affected by drought. The previous year, 1927, had been a time of great stress. Gerhardt had become ill, later diagnosed as having polio. Ottilie undertook his care using German homoeopathic medical books. She wrapped his limbs in sheets alternatively wrung out in hot and cold water which she had first boiled in the copper. The polio left him with a permanent limp. After this Ottilie herself became very ill with pleurisy and had to return to Adelaide for hospitalisation.

Deep Well had become unlivable. Fine red desert sands covered everything, penetrating inside the house, despite closed doors and windows. Dust covered the furniture, beds and floors with a red coating. In the evening sheets had to be removed from the bed so the family could sleep in peace. When they moved to Alice Springs, in 1928, life

The Johannsen family with "Birtle's car" at Hermannsburg in 1924. Even in the dust of the outback, Ottilie and the girls wore spotless white. Ottilie herself wore white stockings and shoes but allowed the younger children more latitude.

Gerhardt Johannsen and Elsa on a rare Sunday excursion in the Dodge utility.

improved. At last Ottilie could plant a garden. She put in rose beds, pansies and a beautiful garden of flowers on the northern side of the house. Date palms, grape vines and fruit trees grew well and provided delicious fruit as well as shade. To supplement the family's income, Ottilie let the two front rooms of the large house to boarders and sold the grapes that grew in her garden in great abundance.

The family maintains that throughout her life Ottilie's Lutheran faith was a comfort and strength and she always said grace in German before every meal. She died in 1959 and was buried in Alice Springs cemetery.

Chinese garden on the King River at Maranboy, N.T., c. 1935.

In the 19th century, Chinese generally lived in communities outside the main settlements. This unidentified group of Chinese dwellings shows extensive garden development.

## CHINESE

Although a large number of Chinese emigrated to Australia, at first there were very few Chinese women. During the 1840s, before the gold rush, Chinese were brought to Australia as cheap labour, then, with the discovery of gold, they flocked into the country. By 1857, over 20 000 had arrived on the Victorian goldfields. After the rush subsided, many subsequently returned home, but those who stayed moved throughout the country. Some turned to vegetable growing, restaurants and many ran country stores.

Comments and reminiscences about Chinese vegetable growers occur all over the country. Often called "Johnny Chinaman", they were misunderstood and often lonely figures in Australian history. In the northern areas many Chinese married or cohabited with Aboriginal women and, in the latter part of the 19th century and early 20th century, some returned to China bringing back with them young Chinese wives under a system of marriage arranged either through marriage brokers or by arranging for payment to poorer families.

Neat Chinese gardens supplied vegetables to many country towns. Workers on goldfields universally relied on Chinese agricultural skill for their fresh fruit and vegetables. The Chinese grew European vegetables but also Chinese cabbage as well as soya beans and ginger. The Chinese vegetable hawker was a common local identity well into the 20th century, and Chinese led the development of market gardens around every city.

Many Chinese leased north Queensland river flats and established the banana industry there in the 1890s.

In the Murrumbidgee-Lachlan rivers district Chinese labourers were employed by station owners wanting workers to carry out ringing or scrubbing.

On arrival, Chinese workers quickly erected tents and a long bark cooking galley.

> "Every man knew his job, and there was no overlapping in method — they could run rings around Europeans."[6]

In the outback areas, lone Chinese workers were in demand as station cooks and gardeners.

> "... we had already a flourishing, well-stocked kitchen garden which was attended to carefully by a yellow pigtailed patient Chinaman ..."[7]

There is little evidence remaining of the interaction between women and early Chinese settlers. According to one historian:

> "two shepherds usually lived together with a hut keeper, sometimes a European shepherd's wife who made the meals and cleared up. Each shepherd managed a separate flock in South Australia, for example from 500 to 1 500."[8]

Chinese procession in Cavanagh Street, Darwin. No women are evident although there is a large number of children.

On the goldfields in Victoria, north-western Australia, Pine Creek, Northern Territory and the Cooktown area, the labourers probably either remained celibate, lived or slept with Aboriginal women or visited prostitutes.

Although there is little written material some pictorial evidence remains to show that a reasonable number of Chinese women had come to Australia by

A rare glimpse of Chinese women in Darwin at the turn of the century.

the 1890s. In north-western Australia and the Cooktown area of Queensland, it was far more common for Aborigines and Chinese to intermarry and Aboriginal surnames today attest to a long and solid Chinese/Aboriginal union. In small towns and stations Chinese gradually met and married European women — often cooks, farm or station maids and workers. At Coochin, the diary of the station owner's son records that a Chinese stockman named Jimmy,

> "lived for many years as a bachelor . . . One day he was sent with the buggy to bring back a new cook. She was not a beauty and Jimmy told my Father there was no danger of anyone running off with her. However, beauty being only skin deep, Jimmy succumbed to her charms and she made him a very good wife and they lived in his cottage at Coochin for many years."[9]

Most country towns would have included famous Chinese identities amongst the early market gardeners, merchants and businessmen. The Northern Territory has a particularly strong Chinese heritage and lengthy Chinese presence in Darwin.

Reminiscences of Chinese women descendants of several generations of Australian-born Chinese in Darwin reveal that customs and traditions relating to pregnancy and childbirth were upheld within the Chinese community until late in the 20th century.

Chinese women traditionally stayed at home and attended the garden although they worked extremely hard carting water and planting vegetables. Lily Ah Toy was born in Darwin in 1917. Her mother, Lindy Moo, was also born in Darwin in the early 1890s. Lily Ah Toy recalls the advice that was given to her and other Chinese women about childbirth:

> "The most important thing, which they have every week is Foojook — dried bean curd, boiled, soak it and put a beaten egg in it and put some rock sugar. This is to be eaten last thing at night. Another thing they have is Dongeue, a root. You boil an egg, rock sugar and the root together and also eat it last thing at night, it helps to nourish the baby. You only had it once a fortnight. They continue to work, hard work.[10]

After the birth it was the custom for the mother to rest for a month, undertaking only light work, such as washing the baby and the nappies. Both the mother and baby's stomachs were bound with very fine cotton material.

A Chinese nursing mother would look after her diet well, eating chicken with green ginger and oil, or pigs' trotters cooked with vinegar and ginger. In most cases Chinese midwives attended the birth. In Darwin these included Hung Yuen and Granny Tye. One unusual and famous woman of the Northern Territory was Sarah Bowman, a Londoner who married Lee Hang Gong, and travelled to Palmerston, in the Northern Territory, to begin a drapery business. Their children were born in the 1880s in Darwin and included Arthur Lee Hang Gong, a mounted policeman who was to travel to Hong Kong for a marriage arranged by a traditional matchmaker.

# GRANNY LUM LOY

## c. 1887–1980

Granny Lum Loy was also known as Lu Moo and Lee Toy Kim. She was one of the many Chinese who came by ship to Darwin from the late 1870s. She was immediately adopted by a Chinese storekeeper and his wife who lived in Darwin. All her life she retained the traditional clothing style which she had worn on arrival: black trousers and cross-over loose top worn with a broadbrimmed hat.

Granny Lum Loy lived well into her 90s and was a familiar sight in Darwin. In her childhood, she mixed widely in the Chinese community, speaking only Chinese, yet she formed many friendships with Aboriginal people whom she respected all her life.

In 1901 Lu Moo married Lum Loy, a Chinese miner. The couple travelled to Pine Creek where a large deposit of wolfram had been found. During this period the Pine Creek area was very busy. It had numerous Chinese shops and vegetable gardens as well as an extensive Chinese shanty town which was occasionally visited by the authorities to inspect the conditions. Lu Moo was a

Granny Lum Loy packing bananas in her garden in 1979.

devout Buddhist and attended the three joss houses in Brocks Creek near Pine Creek, and later, the Chinese temple in Darwin. Her daughter Lizzie Yook Lin was born at a railway siding at Brocks Creek in December 1906.

Lizzie later married a prominent Darwin businessman and they had nine children, all delivered in Darwin by the well-known Chinese midwife, Sarah Lee Hang Gong.

Granny Lum Loy's life centred on business and gardening — the need to be independent and make a living. Initially, after her daughter and family left Darwin to start a business in Katherine, she rented land and single-handedly planted a mango orchard of 200 trees, carrying water from the well and compost from a large pit. It was a prolific enterprise which she harvested herself, sending the fruit to Western Australia. Just before the 1939–45 War Granny Lum Loy sold the mango plantation in order to assist her daughter who had returned to run a cafe in Darwin's Chinatown. At other times in her life, Granny Lum Loy kept chickens and sold the eggs.

Even in her 90s, Granny Lum Loy was an extraordinarily active woman, her black-garbed figure tending her garden of mangoes, guavas, five corners, custard apples, ginger, garlic, bananas, chillies, yams, Chinese melons and bitter melons. At this advanced age, she still regularly walked the distance from her house to the joss house in Darwin.

Granny Lum Loy of Darwin.

Granny Lum Loy wore traditional Chinese clothes and broadbrimmed hat throughout her life. She worked in her garden until her 90s, at one time tending 200 mango trees.

A trapper's wife and children (just visible) outside their bag and brush dwelling on an isolated property in South Australia, 1907.

While vast distances remain between outback properties, radio and telephone communication links now reduce the isolation felt by many women.

# ISOLATION AND COMPANY

O ne factor that was a common experience for all women in remote holdings was the isolation and loneliness they felt — the longing for the company of other women, for conversation and the chance to share experiences. With husbands away for long periods, women could become withdrawn and despondent. Children were the sole companions and there was little opportunity for the stimulation of adult conversation.

In these circumstances occasional callers and visitors provided a lift to the spirits although they were perceived in different ways depending on the circumstances. Unless the family was closely attached to a local group of Aborigines, and had friendly relations, fear would strike a lonely woman if unknown Aborigines approached the house — the era of Aboriginal retaliation for the white invasion and mutual fear continued well into the 20th century. Similarly, callers such as swagmen or hawkers could arouse fear for life and property in women on their own.[1]

In the latter half of the 19th century, a large number of men were moving throughout the country, particularly along the Murray, Murrumbidgee and Lachlan rivers. They were called swagmen, travellers, or sundowners, the latter term referring to the fact that they usually arrived about sundown needing rations or a place to sleep. Their main ports of call were the large stations where there was plenty of work. They would arrive, ask for odd work and receive rations in return which might consist of flour and meat, or sometimes a little sugar and tea. Women alone with small children did not encourage such callers, for fear of the potential consequences. Some were brave, however, and chose to take the offer of extra labour to help with the woodcutting or the carting of water and other manual tasks.

Although the picture, portrayed by Barbara Baynton in her classic book, *Bush Studies*, of the woman shivering in fear underneath the blanket while a lone man roamed the slab house, peeping through the gaps between the planks, might have seemed extreme, such stories, with their violent endings, were extremely prevalent in the bush.

The diary of Elizabeth Tierney, who succeeded in keeping an extensive farm as well as rearing six children after her husband's death, is full of the daily notes relating to farm production, weather and visitors. There is, however, a remarkable entry which records the rumours about the dramatic rampage by Jimmy and Joe Governor and Jackie Underwood, who were involved in massacring Mrs Tierney's neighbours in 1900. The diary is notable for its understatement — a perfect example of a woman who kept her head above water and resolved to face each day as it came. The work had to be done. Nevertheless, her fear comes through in her brief notations:

"*23 Mon* Light rain, did not wash. Mr and Mrs McKay were murdered at Reedy Creek Gulgong by the Blackfellows, the same ones that killed the Newberry family on Friday night. The police & civilians & trackers after them, they are traveling fast. *24 Tues* Fine day. We washed. Retta went for violin lessons. I paid Mr Walshe 11/- for 6 lessons. The Blacks murdered Mrs O'Brien & child & wounded one other woman at Ulan and Casselles on their way to Waller where they intend to kill more. They have killed eight altogether.
*25 Wed* Terribly windy. Katie went down to Johnie's in the morning. One of the blacks, Jackie Underwood, was captured at Leadville all the police & Civilians after the other blacks. China War raging.
*26 Thu* Cloudy like rain. Retta went down to Johnies to get our tea, 20 lbs at 1/6 from Griffiths Bros. I don't care for it. There are over 50 policemen & a lot of civilians & trackers after Jimmie & Joe Governor, the blackfellows & murderers. The Breelong murder which happened on the 20th inst. was the cruelest & worst murder that was ever committed in Australasia, there was four killed with tommighawks & two not expected to live."[2]

As some men drank heavily women were often afraid of unknown callers, and most kept a gun handy. Some were welcome — particularly Afghan or Sikh hawkers. When their camels appeared on the horizon with laden carts, word travelled excitedly. Merchandise of all kinds was offered. Everyone crowded around their cart — the only shop they had the chance to visit.

Despite the rivalry that existed between the squatters and the small selectors, in times of severe strife — robbery, death, or loss of children for example, all families in the district would unite. Because of the employment of numbers of men, the squatter had the capacity to help by organising labour, either to chase a thief, pursue "errant" Aborigines (usually with uncalled for, dire consequences) or search for lost children. Yet even the squatters' children could be so isolated that the sight of a female visitor could be startling. In one record of a pioneering family near Geelong, in Victoria, written in 1842, the wife recalls:

"I was delighted to have the privilege of talking to a lady again; it was more than a year since I had seen one; and my little girl had not words to express her delight and astonishment. The sight of a 'white lubra', as she called her, seemed for a time to take away her speech; but she soon began to question her very closely as to where she came from and whether there were any more like her in the country."[3]

As more settlers came to the bush and built houses within a day or two's ride of each other, neighbours provided great fellowship. Women could visit each other, particularly in times of childbirth or illness and stay for a while. It was a chance to break the normal routine and have a continued stretch of female companionship.

The pensive solitary activity of letter writing which was the only link of friendship for many women in remote areas is evoked by this photograph from an album held in the Australian National Gallery, c. 1869.

Hand-cut and rolled-tin letter holder from the Pioneer Women's Hut collection at Tumbarumba, N.S.W.

# Annie Mary Davis

## (nee Beasley)
## 1873–1954

Annie Mary Beasley was born on board a sailing ship in the Atlantic Ocean in July 1873. After living several years in the United States her family returned to England and four years later left to migrate to Australia, arriving in Launceston on Christmas Eve, 1879.

In 1892, Annie married Thomas Davis at her parents' home in Launceston, where three of their eight children were born. In 1898 they moved to Mt Direction on the east Tamar River where Thomas was a shepherd. Later they moved to Branxholm in north east Tasmania and then to Frankford in 1905 by which time Thomas was a miner and away from home most of the time.

In 1911 Annie moved to Warrentinna outside Branxholm and bought some land on the Warrentinna road. The Hobart Postal Museum records show she was appointed "Receiving Officer Keeper for Warrentinna Post Office ... Salary £7 p.a. plus £6 p.a. for accommodation and light ... & £20 p.a. will be paid for conveyance of mails bet. office and Mara Rail daily."

Affectionately known as "Gran" in the district, Annie ran the post office for more than 20 years, bringing up her children alone, while her husband was away mining. She was also the "bush nurse" delivering babies when the doctor was unavailable.

In 1925 a public phone was installed on the post office verandah, and Annie also ran the Commonwealth Bank agency. Her children grew up and married and her son, Claude, and his wife, Real, lived in the house across the road from the post office. Their houses became half-way houses for travellers from the station to the mill.

The small community at Warrentinna, Tas. The post office is on the far side of the road.

Warrentinna post office. Annie Davis, the postmistress, watches her grandson and another baby, being photographed on the motorbike.

The Davis family at Warrentinna. Annie Davis (on the right) ran the remote post office for 20 years.

## MAIL AND RAIL

Letter writing was the most important means of alleviating loneliness. The mail preserved women's sanity, bringing contact and news of the world. It provided the only means of sending messages to friends and family far away, or ordering supplies from catalogues. It was complemented by contact with the occasional visitor, and much later, the warmly remembered wireless.

As the trains began to criss-cross the country, isolation diminished. In many remote places, people would meet the train even if they had nothing to collect. Talking to the guard would provide quick and instant news and a way of passing something else "down the line".

The mail could be transported by train to the last stop, and then it would have to be carried by vehicles drawn by horses or camels.

Unreliable mail could make isolation all the more severe. One record shows that mail arrived at Birdsville from Marree on 10 April 1886 — but not again until five months later owing to rain.[4] In many areas the Cobb & Co. style mail coach was a familiar and heart-warming sight bringing news from afar.

Whether fortnightly, monthly or six-monthly deliveries of mail, it was always a joyful moment when post offices were established in the area:

"The Post Office was a great boon and kept the stations in touch with the outside world. Garvey was the postmaster for fourteen years in my time at Camboon. His children all read morse code by ear and used to pick up and pass the news. Garvey used to get most annoyed as the children talked to each other during meals tapping out the words in morse, with knife and fork. He could not read by ear."[5]

Aggie Higgins, second postmistress at Margaret River, W.A., 1925.

Transport for the mail, northern Western Australia, 1914.

The first mail car on the run from Holbrook to Jingellic, N.S.W., c. 1924.

## RADIO TELEPHONE, WIRELESS AND THE FLYING DOCTOR SERVICE

Telegraph stations were immensely important in linking people across vast stretches of country.

In 1909, Harry and Alice Woodards were sent from Adelaide to take charge of the remote telegraph station at Yardea, 240 kilometres west of Port Augusta, which had only bush tracks leading to it. The telegraph office was a small stone building of four rooms: a cosy kitchen with a wood stove, a living room, which often served as a room for extra guests, a bedroom, and a store.

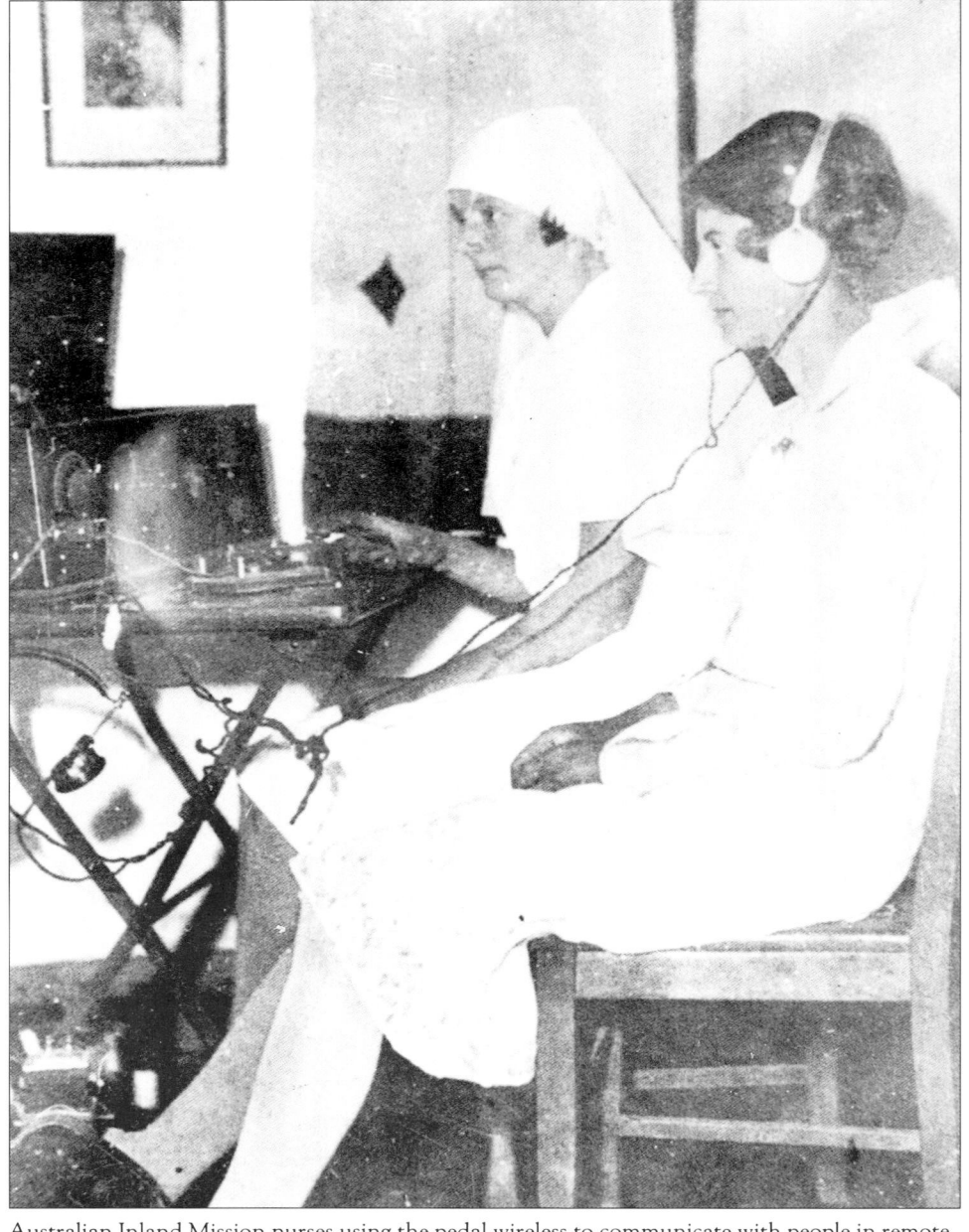

Australian Inland Mission nurses using the pedal wireless to communicate with people in remote areas of central Australia.

Jessie Chalmers at MacDonald Downs station, N.T., 1936.

Each operator had his own way of transmitting, and good telegraphists could tell who was "on the line". The women were often left alone as the men went out on lengthy inspection trips. Linesmen were kept busy repairing and checking the lines which were often cut or damaged. The culprits blamed most often were travellers or Aborigines who had helped themselves when they needed a piece of wire. Telegraph stations were important local institutions — places for travellers to stay overnight. They were also the site of many concerts and dances.

Although there were enthusiastic amateurs who experimented with private wireless transmitters before World War I, during the war experimentation ceased and the development of wireless (or radio) in Australia's bush and outback did not develop until the 1920s and 1930s.

The ability to turn a small set on and to receive voices from afar had a great effect on remote communities. Soon well-known broadcasters became personal friends and world famous singers could be broadcast in the living room. It drew neighbours and friends together, and for women in remote situations, provided a network of "friends".

In country areas, women's programmes were specifically designed to bridge gaps in lonely lives and provide a network of support in times of need.

By the late 1930s radio was the focus of social life in country areas — the means of linking over distance and communicating on women's programmes.

2WG Wagga, the Riverina Broadcasting Company, began in 1932. One of its most important programmes for women was "The Women's Club". News and snippets of interest to women of the district were broadcast regularly. The Club ran a correspondence section and letters from listeners using anonymous pen names were read out telling of events and giving tips and advice. At one time the Club had 26 000 members. Similar women's clubs operated in all states.

Mrs Cundith listening to the first radio transmission from Gympie, Qld, 1921.

Miss Warwick in the transmitting and receiving station of the Flying Doctor Service, Cloncurry, Qld, 1947.

The most serious disadvantage for women in remote outback situations was the lack of access to medical care in times of illness or accident. The problems of childbirth, distances between doctors and the heroic travels of midwives are discussed elsewhere. The establishment of the Flying Doctor Service in the Northern Territory by Rev. John Flynn, not only offered medical facilities to outback people, but indirectly provided a network of social contacts which women found most useful.

The two-way radio network enabled women to hold Country Women's Association meetings over the air. The time slot was irreverently tagged the "Galah Session", but was important in that it enabled women who rarely met but shared common interests to exchange ideas and develop social cohesion.

A christening at the Church of England parsonage, Wyalong, N.S.W., c. 1860.

One of the first buildings to appear in remote communities was the church, providing a social focus for women on Sundays.

# SUNDAYS, DANCES AND SPECIAL OCCASIONS

S unday was universally respected. The "day of rest" was an interlude in the incessant work, strain and labour of the week. It was set aside mainly as a day for religious observance, whether in the open air under a magnificent tree or in a newly-built small community church. After the service, members of the community would take the opportunity to socialise, either visiting each other or enjoying dinners, luncheons or tea in the church hall. Best of all, after the service many families would select an idyllic country spot for a picnic.

On Sundays the very best clothes were produced. It was a time when women could bring out their bonnets, lace collars and cuffs and the elegant, respectable dresses that were usually kept in cupboards during the working week. When women received guests at home work aprons were replaced with heavily embroidered sateen edged with lace.

One of the first buildings to appear in remote communities was the small, primitive church built with communal labour. Many had earthen floors and simple handmade pews consisting of slab benches. On some of the larger stations the workmen and their wives, and nearby poorer settlers, would also assemble.

> "On each Sunday, when the weather permitted, a service was held at a short distance from the house in the open air, under some magnificent gum tree, which was attended by the shepherds on the station, and the few neighbours within reach."[1]

Churches, like the country stores, were very often the formal social centre of a community, but more importantly they acted as the focus of moral fibre — most keenly observed by the women. Women of the district would judge others by their appearance and the degree to which they upheld Christian values — most notably regular attendance at services and conformist social behaviour.

At times the women who found themselves at the mercy of brutal and desperate husbands did not receive support from the clergy. The woman, it seems, within domestic conflict, was never right. In August 1844, Rev. George King wrote to the Bishop of Australia, outlining his concern over a recent case regarding Mrs Lamb, a respectable and well-disposed parishioner:

"Mrs Lamb, with tears in her eyes, besought me not to leave the house until I had persuaded her husband to permit her to go to Church but he would not.

His persecution of his poor wife was so cruel, that she several times abandoned him, bearing on her back and limbs shocking marks of violence: and at length she committed the awful deed of suicide on a Sunday."[2]

Mrs Lamb's suicide attracted a good deal of attention as it was the first in the colony and it is of interest historically simply because it occurred as a clear result of the domestic suffering she was forced to endure and which was passively endorsed by the society in which she found herself. She was refused permission to be buried in the church grounds in accordance with Christian beliefs concerning suicide.

In general, however, the church provided great solace and, equally important, an opportunity for social interaction.

Local residents would club together to raise funds for materials or erect small chapels, or clear a space for a churchyard through communal labour. Preachers moved from place to place, and it was common for a church to be used by preachers from different denominations on alternate Sundays.

A wedding at the remarkable all bark Presbyterian church, Stanthorpe, Qld, 1872.

Sundays were a time for picnics, rest, relaxation and reading. The photographer has included a petrol tin plant stand in this makeshift setting. The young women wear dresses of the same fabric, possibly hand sewn.

Where possible, children walked to church, others were driven in the sulky with their parents. Sunday school would follow afterwards, while the women set out sandwiches or cakes. Once a year many districts observed church anniversary celebrations and these provided opportunities for families to visit each other. On these gala days the food and decorations were prepared well in advance by the women.

Anne Elizabeth Dawkins lived with her parents, Rebecca and Samuel, in the Gawler River district of South Australia. Her recollections, as told to her daughter, are of the chapel anniversary celebrations in the 1870s:

> "For some weeks previous to our great day, all the women were very busy, first sewing, then scrubbing and white washing, to be followed by a great baking of cakes, puddings, poultry and ham, for all kept open house ... Even the spring cart was washed and all the harnesses cleaned by the men and boys, ready for the great occasion."[3]

The anniversary service was followed by guests' visits to the farm. The following Monday was the day of the Tea Meeting, when the chapel doubled as a hall. The pews were moved and the building completely decorated with flowers.

> "Weeks previously the children had gathered masses of wild daisies — white, and yellow and white 'everlastings'. Some of these flowers were then made into wreaths with texts, such as 'Ebenezer' and 'Bethany', spelt out on them. The makers kept secret what texts they were using, and not until the day of the Tea Meeting would the secret be revealed. The remaining everlastings were massed into baskets to which, on Monday morning, were added scarlet pelargoniums. The wreaths too, were dotted here and there with these splashes of red colour. Both baskets and wreaths were then hung up on the hat racks along the walls, or were suspended from the rods which bore the hanging kerosene lamps.
>
> In addition, tubs full of garden flowers were brought in to fill the vases on the trestles."[4]

As soon as the decoration work was done, the women returned home to make a hurried meal, milk the cows and feed the stock before returning for the 4 p.m. Tea. The wives of the eight trustees of the chapel, together with one or two families of the congregation, then took turns in giving the tea or "trays" as it was called.

> "All the food was homemade, and the charm of homemade bread and butter, ham and cakes, brought many visitors from the neighbouring town as well as from the surrounding country congregations. To be a success, the tables had to have been filled three or four times."[5]

Country race meetings or church events often necessitated "bush luncheons". This inviting setting was at Tilba Tilba, N.S.W.

The table has been set, ready for a pleasant outdoor meal, Western Australia, 1910.

*Above and below*: Two family groupings both attending the Landor station picnic races, W.A., 1938.

The women and children of Stuart (now Alice Springs) at the picnic races, c. 1920.

## DANCES AND RACES

The tradition of the country dance, woolshed dance or barn dance began at the very outset of colonial life in Australia, and continues as a living tradition in numerous small communities.

Upon the completion of a communal building or after the annual races dances were held. Excitement and expectation made these important to everyone. They were the main opportunities for courtship, fun and distraction from daily hard work. Guests might stay overnight on neighbouring farms and as on such festive occasions, dancing would often continue all night.

Horse races were not held often. The big race meeting might be held annually or perhaps every three years. In outback areas they were an occasion when *everyone* came to watch.

Photographs show the race meeting was a major social occasion — the women were seated side by side in their best clothes, while to one side, the Aborigines also came to watch.

At Grong Grong, in the Murrumbidgee-Riverina district in the early 1890s, the annual race day was the focus for much excitement:

> "It was an all-bush meeting, just untrained station or farm hacks, piloted by any class of rider that could sit a pigskin. The course was round the back of the hotel, an old wooden building that stood on the side of the present day hotel, and the winning post was right in front of the bar door, and many's the heated debate was settled in the dust between the little gate leading to the railway, and the hotel . . ."

At the races and at the dances that followed, subtle segregation separated gentry from working folk, and black from white.

In the Richmond River district of New South Wales at more formal dances and balls the hall was divided down the middle by a line. One side was for the "silvertails" and the other for the "coppertails" [6] In other areas if this practice began the coppertails often decided to attend no longer.

Until very recently weekly dances in woolsheds, houses and country halls was the only focus for courtship for many shy young couples. As a young woman, Minnie Galvin from Lankey's Creek, New South Wales, went to the local dance where her father played the violin and accordion. Although staying with a neighbour, Mrs Wright, she would ride home each Sunday to see her mother:

"It was on one of these occasions when I reached the top of a hill, Mick Galvin who was riding up the road, travelling in the opposite direction also reached the top of the hill. We both stopped and talked for a while. During the conversation I said, 'There is a dance being held in the Coppabella woolshed on Friday. Are you coming to it? He replied, 'I don't know anyone about here, if I go, would you have the first dance with me?' I said yes. Four years later I married him. He bought a block of land at The Four Mile, and then selected 1609 acres joining Yarrara Station. All our nine children were born while we lived at 'Four Mile'."[7]

In Tumbarumba, New South Wales, dances were popular local entertainment for a century. To music from accordion, violin, mouth organ and piano, couples danced the waltz, schottische, one step, two step and square dance, but only the more daring tried the boompsadaisy or blackbottom.

Members of the Kennedy family of Burra, S.A., enjoyed musical gatherings where they performed with friends, c. 1890.

232

The country dance was a mecca for young men and women. The local hall was simply decorated, women brought a plate and drank cordial. The men were often not so abstemious.

It was a great event and problems of distance or very young families were overcome. One local resident, Edie Hill, recalled that her mother, Frances Jackson, rode sidesaddle all the way from Sharpe's Creek to Tumbarumba to attend the dance. Children were put to sleep on rugs in the cloakroom. Mrs Cuskey played the piano while her baby slept in a drawer nearby.

Sulkies and, later, cars were packed to the limits. The town of Carabost had such popular dances in the late 1920s that Harry Dunn of Tumbarumba cut his Oldsmobile in half and extended the chassis so he could sit eight people in at 2s 6d a time.

For supper women usually "took a plate" and tea was served, or, occasionally, coffee made from coffee essence. Fights and pranks were part of the dances. There was often havoc as horses were switched or jam spread on saddles. The favourite trick was to untie the horses, put the sulky shafts through the fence, and re-tie the horses to the sulky with the fence between.

Mrs Draper, her sister and child, accompanied by Aboriginal women staff at a picnic on Bond Springs station, N.T., c. 1920.

Picnics were always fun. Many photographs were taken with the party toasting or skylarking. Pictured near Alice Springs are the Wilkinson family with Miss Fitzpatrick and Bill Wuttke, between 1921 and 1926.

## PICNICS

Despite the excitement and the anticipation that an approaching country dance or race meeting held, family or community picnics were far more frequently enjoyed as a source of relaxation. Young people often took a small hamper and drinks or a billy can down to a pleasant gully. The outdoor meal was shared while brothers and sisters watched the birds or fish swimming, or caught yabbies. Sunday picnics were a family event. Everyone got in the buggy and went to "a lovely spot" usually near water, with plenty of shade from large trees. In a clearing free of snakes and other insects the family boiled the billy.

There is more photographic evidence of picnics than virtually any other social activity throughout Australia's early pioneering history. It seems that the camaraderie, relaxation of the spirits (and possibly imbibing of them), as well as the compulsory cup of tea provided an occasion deemed so memorable that it had to be recorded. Coastal pioneering communities took the opportunity to picnic at the beach and the nostalgic photographs of the late 19th and early 20th century show incongruously dressed parties, romping freely and enjoying the air and space.

In the late 19th century, stencils were used to make prints in shapes which reflected the subject matter. This entirely appropriate teapot frames a picnic scene in South Australia, c. 1893.

Priscilla Bale was born in Yamba, on the New South Wales coast, in May 1879. At the age of six she went to live with her mother and stepfather at Woodburn and attended the small Woodburn school. She recalled Sunday afternoons spent exploring the scrub near Evans Head. The picture created by reminiscences of the coastal bush at the turn of the century brings regret and longing to many an old-timer. In areas long since replaced by lawns and buildings, there was once open heath and plentiful wild fruit. As a young girl Priscilla Bale gathered wild fruit, geebungs, Five Corners, "as good as chewing gum", wild cherries, raspberries, strawberries, figs, plums, currants, tamarinds and native limes for making drinks. In September the heath was a blaze of colour, grass trees were interspersed with honeysuckle, bottle brush, boronias, small flowers, and in December, Christmas bells by the thousands. Priscilla and her family travelled there by horse and dray leaving at daybreak for picnics. On arrival they would have a billy of tea and some cake and then head into the surf for a paddle. The plentiful fish and oysters were cooked on the open fire.[8]

A very well-dressed group picnic in the grass at Geraldton, W.A., 1890s.

A picnic at Salmon Ponds, Tas., c. 1900. The well-laid picnic cloth has been decorated with ferns for the occasion.

Gathering Western Australian wildflowers, c. 1880. Sundays provided an opportunity for young women to socialise and walk in the bush. The spectacular beauty of "wild gardens" of flowers were often praised in women's diaries of the period.

A picnic beside the Armadale bus, Western Australia, c. 1930.

The arrival of the new "Model T" car meant family outings and picnics for the McNabb and Birkin families in the Victorian mallee district, c. 1924. (*See feature on Clara McNabb, page 102.*)

Mothers throughout the bush worked into the night making presents for the children and decorations for the tree. This photograph, taken at Christmas 1918, shows Mrs Mary Inches with her family at "Laurel Banks", Huon, Tasmania.

## SPECIAL OCCASIONS AND CHRISTMAS

At all major occasions of life — christenings, weddings, Easter or Christmas — communities sought an occasion to get together. Small groups travelled hundreds of kilometres in "sociables", horse-drawn carriages with two seats facing parallel behind, and on arrival sometimes a large tent would be put up to greet family members coming from afar. In the pioneering situations described herein the family itself provided the immediate and primary social group. The family did everything together. In many situations extended families came together. Cousins and distant relations corresponded about the intricacies of daily life and the support and response they received helped them keep up their spirits. It was always possible for a family member to travel and stay with another, comfortably familiar with the general household news.

Anticipating large gatherings, the men would put up a large tent with a table beneath; the women would make a batch of preserved jam, pies, tarts and cakes.

> "Mother attended to the baking, whilst the children were as busy as they could be . . . we got the poultry ready, made plum puddings and custard, mustered and cleaned our crockery, glass, etc., and collected all our things in the dairy, which looked then like anything but a dairy, for it had hardly any milk in it."[9]

Regardless of circumstances families celebrated Christmas in their particular way, on Christmas Eve as in the German tradition or with a midday Christmas feast and toys from Father Christmas or Santa Claus. Hard times did not prevent women from spending weeks secretly working late at night making things by hand so their children would not go without.

> "Molly, who had herself not long outgrown Santa Claus, could not bear the thought of those empty stockings. All night long she worked by the light of a smoky oil lamp, painting rainbow colours on old worn rubber balls, fashioning little toys and covering them with silver paper, making necklaces and bracelets with bright beads taken from milk-jug covers, making toffee and parcelling it up in coloured paper. With the chill, wet dawn, three young people awakened to find stockings fat with mysterious parcels and not all the toys of a millionaire's child would have made them happier that Christmas morning."[10]

Everyone celebrated Christmas one way or another. Although it has always been incongruous in Australia's heat, the English tradition of Christmas with its hot roast and steaming pudding survives to the present. Throughout the country in small bark huts, larger selections, cattle stations and sheep stations, on 25 December, the prevailing principle of "goodwill to all" prevailed. Flour and pudding mix were shared with station hands, and distributed to Aborigines.

Despite their financial circumstances most women attempted to create an atmosphere for their family that recreated and evoked their own childhood Christmases, and this included erecting and decorating a Christmas tree and placing presents around the tree. Homemade decorations festooned the house

Best clothes and a portrait photograph with the cook and the pudding basin. Christmas at Nullagine, W.A., 1906.

and a roasted repast of admirable proportion was expected. As early as 1852, Emily Clark, whose diary of the early years of settlement in South Australia still remains, recalls that after Christmas dinner in heat of over 90 degrees the roast beef and plum pudding had their effect:

> "After dinner we rested in our chambers and did not reunite until tea time, then we took our chairs into the field sat in a little circle trying to play games and singing. There we sat until the stars shone brightly and the wind became cooler when we adjourned to the house, all agreeing, considering the circumstances, we had had a very pleasant day."[11]

Ottilie Johannsen celebrated Christmas in the traditional German manner with her family. The Christ Child brought presents on Christmas Eve and the family opened them then. There was no "Father Christmas". She would send Gerhardt, her husband, or one of the older children out into the creeks to cut down a native pine tree. She painted its small cones silver and gold and made her own decorations from silver paper taken from the lining of tea boxes. Everything was homemade as camel trains were two months apart in making deliveries. She made her own sweets from traditional German recipes and all the presents as well.

Gerhardt carved a rocking horse for the children and a cradle out of three-ply packing boxes. Ottilie made beautiful gingerbread biscuits, the family recalls, and cut these with special tin shapes cut out of kerosene tins. One

At remote Deep Well, south of Alice Springs, Ottilie Johannsen ensured her children had a happy Christmas. Her tree, a casuarina from the creek bed, is decorated with homemade toys and iced biscuits.

Christmas the dust was so bad at Deep Well that the family ate their Christmas dinner under a very large double bed sheet seated at the kitchen table. She had a portable organ (carried there by overland Afghan camel trains) and taught herself to play hymns and carols from a German handbook.

Elsie Henderson (nee Philp) lived for many years in primitive conditions on a sheep property beyond Charleville in Queensland. Her father, James Philp, founded the shipping company Burns Philp and Co. and was later Premier of Queensland. Although she came from an extremely well-placed family, she made the best of difficult circumstances. On the Eve of Christmas 1922, she wrote to her sister May:

"It is very hot and still tonight and I feel as limp as the pillow-slips hanging from the cots. The house is decked for Christmas, but not with flowers as yours will be, for we haven't any. Bill brought in a tree from the sandhill and soft fern fronds from the river bed, which is almost dry now. I did not really want the tree cut — there is so little to be seen of anything green on this brown drought-stricken landscape. But Bill only wants us to have a normal (as possible!) Christmas. The lovely pine scent fills the room and we have gum-nut men and stars of silver lolly paper and the bright parcels you sent are waiting to be opened. Walter, the pet kangaroo, found the box of raisins so had to be banished in disgrace! . . .

Johnny built a manger of bark and stick to-day and I can see the star shining from here. Bill fashioned it from a piece of kerosene tin.

It is all so still and peaceful that one knows that God is in His Heaven this Christmas and that surely it will rain soon and our pastures will be green again.

All is calm . . all is right . .

Good-night my beloved sisters, sleep well, sleep tight!"[12]

Christmas Day, 1906, at Nullagine, W.A.

Mr and Mrs Bradshaw distributing Christmas pudding mix to Aboriginal women and children at Stuart (later Alice Springs), 1902. The children either ate the paste wet or the women cooked it in the ashes of the fire, like damper.

# ENDNOTES

## THE FIRST HOME

1 Harris, Alexander, *The Emigrant Family or The Story of an Australian Squatter*, Smith, Elder & Co., London, 1849, p. 65.
2 Ibid, p. 63.
3 Ibid, p. 66.
4 Ibid, p. 67.
5 Foott, Mrs J., *Sketches of Life in the Bush or Ten Years in the Interior*, Loxton & Co., Sydney, 1878, p. 19.
6 Ibid.
7 Liddy, Anne, in S.A. Speaks: An Oral History of Life in South Australia before 1930, Mortlock Library of South Australiana, ref. 8504, ATB/4/129–4i, Part 1, p. 20.
8 Brown, Judith, and Mullins, Barbara, *Country Life in Pioneer South Australia*, Rigby Publishers, Adelaide, 1977, p. 83.
9 Reddin, Beth, *My Mother Said: An Anecdotal History Concerning South Australia from 1838 to 1910*, published by the author, Adelaide, 1985, p. 78.
10 Thornley, William, *Adventures of an Immigrant in Van Diemen's Land* (first published 1840s), Rigby Publishers, 1973, p. 47.
11 Skemp, John Rowland, *Memories of Myrtle Bank: The Bush-farming Experiences of Rowland and Samuel Skemp in North-Eastern Tasmania 1883–1948*, Melbourne University Press, 1952, p. 43.
12 Kingston, William H. G., *How to Emigrate; or, The British Colonists*, Grant & Griffith, London, 1850, p. 267.
13 Casson, M. R., "Life on the River Murray — One of its Aspects", in Brown, Louise, (ed.), *A Book of South Australia: Women in the First Hundred Years*, Rigby Publishers, Adelaide, 1936.
14 Kingston, William H. G., *How to Emigrate; or, The British Colonists*, Grant & Griffith, London, 1850, p. 267.
15 Freeman, Hilda M., in Niccol, Brenda, (ed.), *Murrumbidgee Memories and Riverina Reminiscences*, published privately, 1985, p. 117.
16 Foott, Mrs J., *Sketches of Life in the Bush or Ten Years in the Interior*, Loxton & Co., Sydney, 1878, p. 85.

## HOUSEKEEPING

1 Elliott, Beatrice, in S.A. Speaks: An Oral History of Life in South Australia before 1930, Mortlock Library of South Australiana, ref. 8601, ATB/13/129–60Ii, p. 39.
2 Notes kept by the Pioneer Women's Hut, Tumbarumba, as part of their regional oral history collection.
3 Minnie Galvin's reminiscences, Pioneer Women's Hut, Tumbarumba.
4 Elliot, Beatrice, in S.A. Speaks: An Oral History of Life in South Australia before 1930, Mortlock Library of South Australiana, ref. 8601, ATB/13/129–601i.
5 Wilson, Ethel, in S.A. Speaks: An Oral History of Life in South Australia before 1930, Mortlock Library of South Australiana, ref. 8619, ATB/23/119–619i, p. 45.
6 O'Reilly, Bernard, *Green Mountains and Cullenbenbong*, W. R. Smith & Paterson, Brisbane, 1949, p. 139.
7 Records of the Pioneer Women's Hut, Tumbarumba. Correspondence between Wendy Hucker and Claude Meredith, storekeeper, 1930s–40s. Recorded 1986.
8 Oral history recorded July 1985, Pioneer Women's Hut, Tumbarumba.
9 Personal correspondence with author.
10 Isaacs, Jennifer, *The Gentle Arts*, Weldon Publishing, 1988.
11 Elizabeth Tierney, unpublished diary, Mitchell Library, Sydney, ML MSS 2721, p. 131.
12 For a discussion of this see Dianne Bell, *Generations*, Penguin, Ringwood, 1988.
13 Haygarth, Henry William, *Recollections of Bush Life in Australia, During a Residence of Eight Years in the Interior*, John Murray, London, 1850, p. 153.
14 *Fearson's Weekly*, 4 January 1879, quoted in Jones, Helen, *In Her Own Name: Women in South Australian History*, Wakefield Press, Cowandilla, 1986, p. 55.
15 Jones, Helen, *In Her Own Name: Women in South Australian History*, Wakefield Press, Cowandilla, 1986, p. 61.
16 Carter, Jan, *Nothing to Spare, Recollections of Australian Pioneering Women*, Penguin, Ringwood, 1981, p. 29.

## FOOD

1 Haygarth, Henry William, *Recollections of Bush Life in Australia, During a Residence of Eight Years in the Interior*, John Murray, London, 1850, pp. 88–89.
2 Reminiscences of Jane Isabella Watts on Kangaroo Island, quoted in Brown, Judith, and Mullins, Barbara, *Country Life in Pioneer South Australia*, Rigby Publishers, Adelaide, 1977, pp. 67–68.
3 O'Reilly, Bernard, *Green Mountains and Cullenbenbong*, W. R. Smith & Paterson, Brisbane, 1949, p. 73.
4 Minnie Galvin's reminiscences, Pioneer Women's Hut, Tumbarumba.
5 Alyce O'Donnell's reminiscences, Pioneer Women's Hut, Tumbarumba.
6 Reminiscences of Mount Barker, 5 November 1843, quoted in Kwan, Elizabeth, *Living in South Australia: A Social History*, Vol. 1, South Australian Government Printer, Adelaide, 1979, p. 26.
7 Boothby, Mary, "Memories of My Bush Life", in *Journal of the Historical Society of South Australia*, No. 12, 1984, p. 128.
8 Liddy, Anne, S.A. Speaks: An Oral History of Life in South Australia before 1930, Mortlock Library of South Australiana, ref. 8504, ATB/4/129–4i, p. 17.
9 Elliott, Beatrice C., in S.A. Speaks: An Oral History of Life in South Australia before 1930, Mortlock Library of South Australiana, ref. 8601, ATB/13/129–601i, p. 15.
10 Thornleigh, William, in Mills, John, (ed.), *Adventures of an Immigrant in Van Diemen's Land* (first published 1840s), Rigby Publishers, Adelaide, 1973, p. 48.
11 Conigrave, Mrs J. Fairfax, *My Reminiscences of the Early Days*, Brokenshaw & Shaw Ltd, Perth, 1938. p. 61.
12 Ibid.
13 Foott, Mrs J., *Sketches of Life in the Bush or Ten Years in the Interior*, Loxton & Co., Sydney, 1878.

## SHOPPING LONG DISTANCE

1 Rajkowski, Pamela, *In the Tracks of the Camelmen: Outback Australia's Most Exotic Pioneers*, Angus & Robertson, Sydney, 1987.
2 O'Reilly, Bernard, *Green Mountains and Cullenbenbong*, W. R. Smith & Paterson, Brisbane, 1949.
3 Jack Miller's reminiscences, Pioneer Women's Hut, Tumbarumba.
4 Minnie Galvin's reminiscences, Pioneer Women's Hut, Tumbarumba.
5 O'Reilly, Bernard, *Green Mountains and Cullenbenbong*, W. R. Smith & Paterson, Brisbane, 1949, p. 79.
6 Dunstan, Martin, *Willunga Town and District, 1901–1925*, Lynton Publications Pty Ltd, Blackwood, 1978.

## CHILDBIRTH, CHILDHOOD AND SCHOOL

1 Starke, A. M. "Coral", in S.A. Speaks: An Oral History of Life in South Australia before 1930, Mortlock Library of South Australiana, ref. 8606, ATB/13/129–606i, p. 10.
2 Waterhouse, Kathleen, Somerville Oral History Collection, Mortlock Library of South Australiana, ref. OH33.
3 Ibid.
4 Ibid.
5 Carter, Jan, *Nothing to Spare: Recollections of Australian Pioneering Women*, Penguin, Ringwood, 1981.
6 From the diary of Emily Churchward, extracts of which were published in McDonald, Stella, *In Paths Directed*, Investigator Press, Adelaide, 1984.
7 Boothby, Mary, "Memories of My Bush Life", in *Journal of the Historical Society of South Australia*, No. 12, 1984, p. 134.
8 Ibid.
9 Freeman, Hilda M., in Niccol, Brenda, (ed.), *Murrumbidgee Memories and Riverina Reminiscences*, published privately, 1985, p. 116.
10 Brown, Judith, and Mullins, Barbara, *Country Life in Pioneer South Australia*, Rigby Publishers, Adelaide, 1977, p. 72.
11 Minnie Galvin's reminiscences, Pioneer Women's Hut, Tumbarumba.
12 Carter, Jan, *Nothing to Spare: Recollections of Australian Pioneering Women*, Penguin, Ringwood, 1981.
13 O'Reilly, Bernard, *Green Mountains and Cullenbenbong*, W. R. Smith & Paterson, Brisbane, 1949, p. 82.
14 Sizer, Heather, *Yet Still They Live, Wirrabara's Story*, Lutheran Publishing House, Adelaide, 1974, p. 72.
15 Minnie Galvin's reminiscences, Pioneer Women's Hut, Tumbarumba.
16 Freeman, Hilda M., in Niccol, Brenda, (ed.), *Murrumbidgee Memories and Riverina Reminiscences*, published privately, 1985, p. 117.

## WOMEN'S WORK OUTSIDE THE HOME

1 Susan Hunt in 1986 produced an excellent analysis of women in north west Australia — Susan Hunt, *Spinifex and Hessian: Women in North West Australia 1860–1900*, University of Western Australia Press, 1986. As well, Barbara James, *No Man's Land*, Collins, 1989, is an excellent work on key women in the history of the Northern Territory.
2 Cited in Nitwits and Beaumont, *Kangaroo Valley Historical Society and Hampden Bridge Museum Park Trust's Pioneer Farm and Historical Settlement in the Beautiful Kangaroo Valley, N.S.W.*, 1975, p. 19.
3 Boothby, Mary, "Memories of My Bush Life", in *Journal of the Historical Society of South Australia*, No. 12, 1984, p. 128.
4 O'Reilly, Bernard, *Green Mountains and Cullenbenbong*, W. R. Smith & Paterson, Brisbane, 1949.
5 MacKeith, Frances, (ed.), *Letters from Laura: A Bush Schoolmaster in Cape York Peninsular 1892–1896*, James Cook University, Townsville, 1987.
6 Kwan, Elizabeth, *Living in South Australia: A Social History*, Vol. 2, South Australian Government Printer, Adelaide, 1979, p. 15.
7 Kwan, Elizabeth, *Living in South Australia: A Social History*, Vol. 1, South Australian Government Printer, Adelaide, 1979, p. 29.
8 Richards, Eric, *The Flinders History of South Australia: Social History*, Wakefield Press, South Australia, 1986, p. 530, footnote 27.
9 Conigrave, Mrs J. Fairfax, *My Reminiscences of the Early Days: Personal Incidents on a Sheep and Cattle Run in South Australia*, Brokenshaw & Shaw, Perth, 1938, pp. 59–60.
10 Brunato, Madeleine, (ed.), *South Australian Scrapbook: Glimpses of Colourful People and Events*, Rigby Publishers, Adelaide, 1979.
11 Watts, Jane Isabella, *Family Life in South Australia Fifty Three Years Ago, Dating from October 1837*, W. K. Thomas & Co., Adelaide, 1890, pp. 98–99.
12 James, Barbara, *Women of the North, Australian Women's Diary*, 1988.
13 See account of May Steele in *The Stockman*, in the chapter, "On The Track", by Marie Mahood, Lansdowne Press, Sydney, 1984, p. 111.
14 Ibid., p. 110.
15 McGrath, Ann, *Born in the Cattle: Aborigines in Cattle Country*, Allen & Unwin, Sydney, 1987, p. 51.
16 Ibid., p. 62.

## OUTSIDERS

1 Brown, Judith, and Mullins, Barbara, *Country Life in Pioneer South Australia*, Rigby Publishers, Adelaide, 1977, p. 191.
2 Ibid.
3 Kerr, John *Pioneer Pageant: A History of the Pioneer Shire*, Pioneer Shire Council, Mackay, 1980, p. 83.
4 Ibid., p. 88, footnote 17, MM 6.11.80.
5 Sizer, Heather, *Yet Still They Live: Wirrabara's Story*, Lutheran Publishing House, Adelaide, 1974, p. 104.
6 Freeman, Hilda M., in Niccol, Brenda, (ed.), *Murrumbidgee Memories and Riverina Reminiscences*, published privately, 1985, p. 109.

7 Boothby, Mary, "Memories of My Bush Life", in *Journal of the Historical Society of South Australia*, No. 12, 1984, p. 128.
8 Rolls, Eric, "New Guests: The Chinese in Australia", in Foss, Paul, (ed.), *Island in the Stream*, Pluto Press, Sydney, 1988, p. 86.
9 Bell, F. M., Camboon Reminiscences 1904–21, unpublished, John Oxley Library, Brisbane, ref. OM83–24, p. 44.
10 Moran, Irene, and Hanckel, Jenny, *Rain or Shine, She Walks Everywhere: Territory Births 1888–1938*, Childbirth Education Association, Darwin, 1988, p. 5.

## ISOLATION AND COMPANY

1 See Baynton, Barbara, *Bush Studies*, Angus & Robertson, Sydney, 1985.
2 Elizabeth Tierney, unpublished diary, Mitchell Library, Sydney, ML MSS 2721.
3 Quoted in Taylor, Peter, *Station Life in Australia: Pioneers and Pastoralists*, Allen & Unwin, Sydney, 1988.
4 Litchfield, Lois, *Marree and the Tracks Beyond in Black and White*, published by the author, Gillingham Printers, Adelaide, 1983, p. 28.
5 Bell, F. M., Camboon Reminiscences 1904–1921, unpublished manuscript, John Oxley Library, ref. OM83–24, p. 11.

## SUNDAYS, DANCES AND SPECIAL OCCASIONS

1 Watts, Jane Isabella, *Family Life in South Australia: Fifty Three Years Ago, Dating from October 1837*, W. K. Thomas & Co., Adelaide, 1890, p. 98.
2 Rumley, Hilary, "A Missionary's Moral Burden: A Perspective on the Problems of Women in Fremantle in the Early 1840s", in *The Push from the Bush: A Bulletin of Social History*, No. 16, Oct. 1983, pp. 33–34.
3 Reddin, Bette, *My Mother Said: An Anecdotal History Concerning South Australia from 1838 to 1910*, published by the author, Hyde Park Press, Adelaide, 1985, p. 43.
4 Ibid., p. 46.
5 Ibid., pp. 46–47.
6 Oral history collected from Priscilla Bale at the age of 100 in 1979, from records held by Marcia Ritchie and the Richmond River Historical Society, recalling a ball at Woodburn.
7 Minnie Galvin's reminiscences, Pioneer Women's Hut, Tumbarumba.
8 Oral history collected from Priscilla Bale at the age of 100 in 1979, from the records held by Marcia Ritchie and the Richmond River Historical Society.
9 Margaret May's reminiscence of the 1840s, quoted in Kwan, Elizabeth, *Living in South Australia*, Vol. 1, South Australian Government Printer, p. 31.
10 O'Reilly, Bernard, *Green Mountains and Cullenbenbong*, W. R. Smith & Paterson, Brisbane, 1949, p. 76.
11 Kwan, Elizabeth, *Living in South Australia*, Vol. 1, South Australian Government Printer, Adelaide, 1979, p. 44.
12 An extract from a letter to Miss May Philp from her sister Mrs Elsie Henderson. Collated by Mary Brice, her daughter.

# BIBLIOGRAPHY

Adams, Carol, *Ordinary Lives: A Hundred Years Ago*, Virago, London, 1982.

Addison, Susan, and McKay, Judith, *A Good Plain Cook; An Edible History of Queensland*, Boolarong Publications, Brisbane, 1985.

Affleck, Arthur H., *The Wandering Years*, Longmans, Melbourne, 1964.

Barker, Charles John, Esq., *Sydney and Melbourne; with remarks on the Present State and Future Prospects of New South Wales, and Practical Advice to Emigrants of Various Classes: to which is added A Summary of the Route Home by India and Egypt*, Smith, Elder & Co., London, 1845.

Baynton, Barbara, *Bush Studies*, Angus & Robertson, Sydney, 1985.

Bell, Dianne, *Generations*, Penguin, Ringwood, 1988.

Bell, F. M., Camboon Reminiscences 1904–21, unpublished, John Oxley Library, Brisbane, ref. OM83–24.

Berry, D. W., and Gilbert, S. H., *Pioneering Building Techniques in South Australia*, Gilbert Partners, Adelaide, 1981.

Brown, Judith (text), and Mullins, Barbara (photographs), *Country Life in Pioneer South Australia*, Rigby Publishers, Adelaide, 1977.

Brown, Louise (ed.), *A Book of South Australia: Women in the First Hundred Years*, Rigby Publishers, Adelaide, 1936.

Brunato, Madeleine (ed.), *South Australian Scrapbook: Glimpses of Colourful People and Events*, Rigby Publishers, Adelaide, 1979.

Burcher, Honour C., *Pioneers and their Better Halves, or Seven Generations of Women in Australia*, Boolarong Publications, Caloundra, 1985.

Burt, Alison (ed.), *The Colonial Cook Book for the Many as well as the "Upper Ten Thousand": The Recipes of a By-gone Australia*, Paul Hamlyn Pty Ltd, Sydney, 1970.

Cannon, Michael, *Life in the Country: Australia in the Victorian Age*, Currey O'Neil Ross, Melbourne, 1973.

Carter, Jan, *Nothing to Spare: Recollections of Australian Pioneering Women*, Penguin, Ringwood, 1981.

Conigrave, Mrs J. Fairfax, *My Reminiscences of the Early Days*, Brokenshaw & Shaw Ltd, Perth, 1938.

Constitutional Museum, *South Australia 1855: Historical Essays and Teachers' Handbook*, A Come Out Project, Constitutional Museum, April, 1981.

Cowan, Peter (ed.), *A Faithful Picture: The Letters of Eliza and Thomas Brown at York in the Swan River Colony, 1841–1852*, Fremantle Arts Press, Fremantle, 1977.

Czernezkyi, W. (ed.), *Pekina Century and Beyond*, Griffin Press, Adelaide, 1974.

Dunstan, Martin, *Willunga Town and District 1901–1925*, Lynton Publications, Blackwood, 1978.

Eden, Charles H., *My Wife and I in Queensland: An Eight Years' Experience in the Above Colony, with some Account of Polynesian Labour*, Longmans, Green & Co., London, 1872.

Eldershaw, Flora (ed.), *The Peaceful Army: A Memorial to the Pioneer Women of Australia*, Women's Executive Committee and Advisory Council of Australia's 150th Anniversary Celebrations, Sydney, 1938.

Foott, C. H., Letter from C. H. Foott to Mr McKinnon concerning some of his mother's verses, and then reminiscences of station life, unpublished, John Oxley Library, Brisbane, ref. OM81–37.

Foott, Mrs J., *Sketches of Life in the Bush or Ten Years in the Interior*, Loxton & Co., Sydney, 1878.

Foss, Paul (ed.), *Island in the Stream: Myths of Place in Australian Culture*, Pluto Press, Sydney, 1988.

Gilbert, Mrs John, unpublished diary extract, Mortlock Library of South Australiana.

Hamilton, J. C., *Pioneering Days in Western Victoria: A Narrative of Early Station Life*, Exchange Press, Melbourne, 1981.

Harris, Alexander, *The Emigrant Family or, The Story of an Australian Squatter*, Smith, Elder & Co., London, 1849.

Harris, Alexander, *Settlers and Convicts or, Recollections of Sixteen Years' Labour in the Australian Backwoods by an Emigrant Mechanic*, C. Cox, London, 1847.

Haygarth, Henry William, *Recollections of Bush Life in Australia, During a Residence of Eight Years in the Interior*, John Murray, London, 1850.

Hensel, Brenda (compiled by), *Life on the Range: A Collection of Reminiscences from Early Avenue Range Residents*, published by the Community of Avenue Range, Naracoorte, 1986.

Hobden, Jim (ed.), *Tamworth: A Peep at our Yesteryears*, A Tamworth Historical Society Publication, Tamworth.

Hodgson, Christopher Pemberton, *Reminiscences of Australia, with Hints on the Squatter's Life*, W. N. Wright, London, 1846.

Hood, John, *Australia and the East: Being a Journal Narrative of a Voyage to New South Wales in an Emigrant Ship: with a Residence of some Months in Sydney and the Bush, and the Route Home by way of India and Egypt in the Years 1841 and 1842*, John Murray, London, 1843.

Hunt, Susan, *Spinifex and Hessian: Women in North West Australia 1860–1900*, University of Western Australia Press, 1986.

James, Barbara, *No Man's Land*, Collins, 1989.

Johnston, Douglas, *Rich Heritage: The Story of Eureka and its People*, Kyogle, 1987.

Jones, Alan, *Snowtown: the First Century*, Snowtown Centenary Committee, Adelaide, 1978.

Jones, Helen, *In Her Own Name: Women in South Australian History*, Wakefield Press, Cowandilla, 1986.

Kerr, John, *Pioneer Pageant: A History of the Pioneer Shire*, Pioneer Shire Council, Mackay, 1980.

Kingston, Beverley (ed.), *The World Moves Slowly: A Documentary History of Australian Women*, Cassell, Victoria, 1977.

Kingston, William H. G., *How to Emigrate; or, The British Colonists*, Grant & Griffith, London, 1850.

Kwan, Elizabeth, *Living in South Australia: A Social History*, Vol. 1, *From Before 1836 to 1914*; Vol. 2, *After 1914*, South Australian Government Printer, Adelaide, 1979.

Litchfield, Lois, *Marree and the Tracks Beyond in Black and White, Commemorating the Centenary of Marree 1883–1983*, published by the author, Gillingham Printers, Adelaide, 1983.

McCord, Melissa, *Outback Women*, Doubleday, Sydney, 1986.

McDonald, Stella, *In Paths Directed*, Investigator Press, Adelaide, 1984.

MacGillivray, Leith G., Land and People: European Land Settlement in the South East of South Australia, 1840–1940, unpublished PhD thesis, History Department, University of Adelaide, 1982.

McGrath, Ann, Born in the Cattle: Aborigines in Cattle Country, Allen & Unwin, Sydney, 1987.

MacKeith, Frances (ed.), Letters from Laura: A Bush Schoolmaster in Cape York Peninsula 1892–1896, James Cook University, Townsville, 1987.

McKerrow, Helen, Over to You: The First 25 years of School of the Air in North West Queensland, Mt Isa Parents & Citizens Association Publishers, Mt Isa, 1985.

McMurchy, Megan, et al., For Love or Money: A History of Women and Work in Australia, Penguin, Ringwood, 1983.

McQueen, Humphrey, Social Sketches of Australia 1888–1975, Penguin, Ringwood, 1978.

May, Dawn, From Bush to Station: Aboriginal Labour in the North Queensland Pastoral Industry 1861–1897, James Cook University, Townsville, 1983.

Merritt, Alan, and O'Brien, Carolyn, The Striding Years: Squatters and Selectors in 19th Century Australia, CCH Australia Ltd, North Ryde, 1985.

Meredith, Mrs Charles, Notes and Sketches of New South Wales, John Murray, London, 1844.

Mills, John (ed.), Adventures of an Immigrant in Van Diemen's Land (first published 1840s), Rigby Publishers, Adelaide, 1973.

Moran, Irene, and Hanckel, Jenny, Rain or Shine, She Walks Everywhere: Territory Births 1888–1938, Childbirth Education Association, Darwin, 1988.

Morphett, Geo. C. (ed.), Mrs David Randall's Reminiscences, Pioneers Association of Australia, South Australia, 1939.

Nandewar Historical Society, Early Settlers in the Nandewars: Notes by Nandewar Historical Society, Vol. 1, Barraba, 1968.

Niccol, Brenda (ed.), Murrumbidgee Memories and Riverina Reminiscences, published privately, 1985.

Nitwits and Beaumont, Kangaroo Valley Historical Society and Hampden Bridge Museum Park Trust's Pioneer Farm and Historical Settlement in the Beautiful Kangaroo Valley, N.S.W., 1975.

O'Reilly, Bernard, Green Mountains and Cullenbenbong, W. R. Smith & Paterson, Brisbane, 1949.

Petrie, Constance Campbell, Tom Petrie's Reminiscences of Early Queensland (first published 1904), Lloyd O'Neil, Brisbane, 1975.

### Periodicals

Atkinson, Alan, "Women Publicans in 1838", in The Push from the Bush: A Bulletin of Social History, No. 8, 1980.

Aveling, Marian, "Gender in Early New South Wales Society", in The Push from the Bush: A Bulletin of Social History, No. 24, 1987.

Boothby, Mary, "Memories of My Bush Life" (introduced and arranged by Margaret Knox) in Journal of the Historical Society of South Australia, No. 12, 1984.

Byrne, Paula-Jane, "Women and the Criminal Law: Sydney 1810–1821", in The Push from the Bush: A Bulletin of Social History, No. 21, 1985.

Carisbrooke, Donald, "Immigrants in the Bush", in The Push from the Bush: A Bulletin of Social History, No. 5, 1979.

Earnshaw, Beverley, "The Colonial Children", in The Push from the Bush: A Bulletin of Social History, No. 9, 1981.

Gregory, Jenny, "The Gallops of Dalkeith: A Re-examination of a 'Pioneer' Family", in The Push from the Bush: A Bulletin of Social History, No. 22, 1986.

Hawkins, Mrs Elizabeth, "Journey from Sydney to Bathurst in 1822", in Journal of the Royal Australian Historical Society, Vol. IX, Pt IV, 1923.

Rumley, Hilary, "A Missionary's Moral Burden: A Perspective on the Problems of Women in Fremantle in the Early 1840s", in The Push from the Bush: A Bulletin of Social History, No. 16, 1983.

Sissons, D. C. S., "Karayuki-San: Japanese Prostitutes in Australia 1887–1916", Historical Studies, Vol. 17, No. 68, 1977.

### Oral History

Elliott, Beatrice, S.A. Speaks: An Oral History of Life in South Australia before 1930, Mortlock Library of South Australiana, ref. 8601.

Liddy, Anne, S.A. Speaks: An Oral History of Life in South Australia before 1930, Mortlock Library of South Australiana, ref. 8504.

Plush, Rhoda, S.A. Speaks: An Oral History of Life in South Australia before 1930, Mortlock Library of South Australiana, ref. 8615.

Starke, A. M. "Coral", S.A. Speaks: An Oral History of Life in South Australia before 1930, Mortlock Library of South Australiana, ref. 8606.

Waterhouse, Kathleen, Somerville Oral History Collection, Mortlock Library of South Australiana, ref. OH33.

Wilson, Ethel, S.A. Speaks: An Oral History of Life in South Australia before 1930, Somerville Oral History Collection, Mortlock Library of South Australiana, ref. 8619.

Ragless, Margaret E., Dust Storms in China Teacups: Ragless Family Heritage in Australia, published in co-operation with the Ragless Reunion Committee, 1988.

Rajkowski, Pamela, In the tracks of the Camelmen: Outback Australia's Most Exotic Pioneers, Angus & Robertson, Sydney, 1987.

Reddin, Bette, My Mother Said: An Anecdotal History concerning South Australia from 1838 to 1910, published by the author, Hyde Park Press, Adelaide, 1985.

Richards, Eric (ed.), The Flinders History of South Australia: Social History, Wakefield Press, South Australia, 1986.

Ryan, Maurice (ed.), The Story of a North Coast City — Lismore, Currawong Press, Sydney, 1979.

Sawrey, Hugh, et al., The Stockman: Australian Outback Heritage, Lansdowne, Sydney, 1984.

Sizer, Heather, Yet Still They Live: Wirrabara's Story, Lutheran Publishing House, Adelaide, 1974.

Skemp, John Rowland, Memories of Myrtle Bank: The Bush-farming Experiences of Rowland and Samuel Skemp in North-Eastern Tasmania 1883–1948, Melbourne University Press, 1952.

Stone, Derrick I., and Garden, Donald S., Squatters and Settlers, Popular Books, French's Forest, 1984.

Taylor, Peter, Station Life in Australia: Pioneers and Pastoralists, Allen & Unwin, Sydney, 1988.

Thanemann, H. E., Tell the White Man: The Life Story of an Aboriginal Lubra, Collins, London, 1949.

TIERNEY, ELIZABETH, unpublished diary, Mitchell Library, Sydney, ML MSS 2721.

TOWLER, DAVID J., *A Fortunate Locality: A History of Noarlunga & District*, published by the city of Noarlunga, Peacock Publications, Kent Town, 1986.

UNSTEAD, R. J., *Pioneer Home Life in Australia*, Henderson, Melbourne, 1978.

WALKER, J., *The History of Bundaberg: A Typical Queensland Agricultural Settlement*, Gordon & Gotch, Brisbane, 1890 (republished 1977).

WALKER, MURRAY, *Pioneer Crafts of Early Australia*, Macmillan, 1978.

WARBURTON, ELIZABETH (ed.), *Speaking of the Past: Voices of South Australia*, The Corporation of the City of Burnside, Adelaide, 1986.

WATSON, CATHERINE (ed.), *Books and All: An Oral History of Farming in Victoria*, Friends of the Earth, Collingwood, 1984.

WATTS, JANE ISABELLA, *Family Life in South Australia, Fifty Three Years Ago, Dating from October 1837*, W. K. Thomas & Co., Adelaide, 1890, Australiana Facsimile Editions No. 205, Libraries Board of South Australia, Adelaide, 1978.

WEIDENHOFER, MAGGIE (ed.), *Colonial Ladies*, Currey O'Neil Ross, South Yarra, 1985.

WHITE, ISOBEL, et al., *Fighters and Singers*, Allen & Unwin, Sydney, 1985.

WHITELOCK, DEREK (ed.), *Aspects of South Australian History*, Publication 49, Department of Adult Education, University of Adelaide, 1976.

WILLIAMS, FRED, *Written in the Sand: A History of Fraser Island*, Jacaranda Press, Sydney, 1982.

WILLIAMS, MARGARET, unpublished diary, John Oxley Library, Brisbane, ref. OM81–126.

YOUNG, GORDON, et al., *The Barossa Survey*, Vol. 1, A Final Report of a Research Project by the School of Architecture, S.A. Institute of Technology, and the Department of History, Adelaide College of Advanced Education, for the Australian Heritage Commission, 1977.

# ACKNOWLEDGEMENTS

RESEARCH: Martin Thomas, Wendy Hucker
TYPING AND ADMINISTRATIVE ASSISTANCE: Meredith Aveling, Carmel Pepperell, Martin Thomas
PICTURE RESEARCH: Carmen Ky

Many individuals, including Kylie Winkworth and Barbara James, assisted with information during the research and hunt for photographs.

Particular thanks is due to the Pioneer Women's Hut at Tumbarumba, N.S.W. and Wendy Hucker for access to photographs, oral histories and records as well as the opportunity to photograph items in their unique collection.

My grateful thanks to the hardworking staff of public libraries and resource collections used during research. These include: John Blakeman, Old Timers Folk Museum, Alice Springs; Gary Corbett, Broken Hill Regional Gallery; Alison Culpit and Peter Mercer, Tasmanian Museum and Art Gallery, Hobart; Robyn Eastley, State Archives Office of Tasmania, Hobart; Leslie Ewan and Francis McCacknie, Adelaide House Museum, Alice Springs; Helen Innes, Australian National Gallery, Canberra; Lorenzo Iozzi, Royal Historical Society of Victoria, Melbourne; Leslie Keyes and Robin South, Battye Library, Perth; Ken Leckenby, Royal Flying Doctor Service, Brisbane; Michael Loos, State Reference Library of N.T., Darwin; Ros McCormack and Robert NcNaught, John Oxley Library, Brisbane; Euan McGillivray and Matthew Nickson, Museum of Victoria, Melbourne; Judith McRae, Museum of Queensland, Brisbane; Esther Robinson, National Library of Australia, Canberra; Elizabeth Rose, Alice Springs Public Library; Brian Shepherd, Museum of Childhood, Subiaco; Chris Torlach, Conservation Commission, Alice Springs; Judith White, Stanton Library, North Sydney.

During my stay as writer-in-residence, the staff of the State Library of South Australia and the Mortlock Library of South Australiana, in particular Elizabeth Ho, were extremely helpful with research. Christine Finnimore also assisted greatly with South Australian research.

Copyright permissions were handled by Joan Macfarlane of "Quotes". My thanks to her as well as authors, publishers and copyright owners who agreed to my request to use quotations.

Several historical collections deserve special mention and thanks. The Woolpack Inn Museum at Holbrook and the Pioneer Farm Museum, Kangaroo Valley, each gave permission to photograph their domestic utensils. Carol and Nick Dettmann of Jamberoo also unearthed some significant early items for photography including kerosene tin buckets and a wooden wheelbarrow.

The pool of information which formed the basis for this book was provided not only from research but also extensive correspondence. My thanks to the many women (mainly) who wrote with information or helped in other ways. These include: Mrs H. Ashford, Scone, N.S.W.; Mrs Elizabeth Binns, Toowoomba, Qld; Mr P. Bowling, King Island, Tas.; Mrs M. Brice, Toowoomba, Qld; Mrs A. Bucknall, Maryborough, Vic.; Mrs N. Corcoran, Barrellan, N.S.W.; Mr J. Cox, Casino, N.S.W.; Mrs G. Dundon, Gosford, N.S.W.; Miss I. Fenton, Beaufort, Vic.; Ms Beverley Hocking, Adelaide, S.A.; Miss R. Johnson, Broken Hill, N.S.W.; Mr R. J. Laver, Kadina, S.A.; Ms Linda Looney, East Geelong, Vic.; Mrs S. McDonald, Brighton, Vic.; Mrs Lal Mills, Bulimba, Qld; Mrs M. Plantinga, Portland, Vic.; Mrs Rowena Radford, Lawnton, Qld; Ms Marcia Ritchie, Paddington, N.S.W.; Miss Gwen Treasure, Como, W.A.

My thanks also to designer Susan Kinealy for her evocative and sympathetic treatment of the subject and to Deborah Nixon for thorough, thoughtful and painless editing of the manuscript. Lee Chittick contributed photographs of the Kangaroo Valley historic objects and my thanks especially to Carmen Ky for the colour photographs designed to enhance the impact and mood of the text. I owe a sincere debt of gratitude to Meredith Aveling and Martin Thomas for keeping the whole project going, and to my family for continued interest and long-time support.

# PROFILES OF INDIVIDUAL WOMEN

The individual profiles throughout the text were compiled from family records, written histories and interviews. My thanks to the following for assistance in this:

JESSIE MILLER: Lorraine Mitchell, Hackett, A.C.T.;   ISOBEL VIOLET PRICE: Pearl Powell, Alice Springs, N.T.;   JANE O'REILLY: Peter O'Reilly, Lamington Plateau, Qld;   FLORENCE BILTON: Bette Bilton, Maryborough, Vic.;   MATTICK FAMILY: Nancy Howard, Mudgee, N.S.W.;   JANE KELL: Mrs M. Johnston, Maffra, Vic.;   CLARA ELIZABETH ELLEN McNABB: Florence Beaton, Carwarp, Vic.;   MARY JANE COBDEN: Wendy Hucker, Pioneer Women's Hut, Tumbarumba, N.S.W.;   ELIZABETH McCALLUM: Mrs R. McCallum, Seaford, S.A.;   BETTE BILTON: Bette Bilton, Maryborough, Vic.;   LOTTE SULLIVAN: Mrs M. Johnston, Maffra, Vic.;   DOROTHY MAGUIRE: Mrs E. Paterson, Rivett, A.C.T.;   EDITH MAY LAVER: Robert Laver, Adelaide, S.A.;   GLADYS BAUER: Gladys Bauer, Blackall, Qld;   MARIE OTTILIE JOHANNSEN: Mrs Mona Byrne, Alice Springs, N.T.;   GRANNY LUM LOY: Barbara James, Darwin, N.T.;   ANNIE MARY DAVIS: Carol Byron, Launceston, Tas.

# NOTES ON ILLUSTRATIONS

While every effort has been made to obtain permission from copyright holders and to contact the owners of original material, the publishers would be pleased to hear from anyone who has not been duly acknowledged.

These notes supplement the information contained in the captions. They include, as necessary, the details required by holding institutions.

**2** ML (SSL:M B43517); **8** BL (67376P); **10** Mus Childhood (P86.1); **11** courtesy Rowena Radford; **12** *top*: RHS Vic, *bottom left*: ML (SSL:M B44999), *bottom right*: OPHL; **14** BL (198P); **15** *top*: NLA, *bottom left*: PWH; **16** NLA; **17** NLA; **20** Mitchell; **21** Oxley (22161); **22** NTA; **23** *top*: OPH; **25** Oxley (48302); **26** *left*: Cons Comm (Powell-Price Collection); **27** Cons Comm (Powell-Price Collection); **28** *bottom*: Cons Comm (Powell-Price Collection); **31** *top*: BL (67140P), *bottom*: NTA; **32** BL (26140P); **33** Oxley (163919); **34** *top*: NLA (LC Ball Collection), *bottom*: Oxley (13101); **35** *top*: NLA (Hick's Collection), *bottom*: Oxley (18247); **38** *top*: Tyrell Collection, MAAS, *bottom*: Holbrook; **40** PWH; **42** *bottom*: GL; **43** *top*: Nancy Howard Collection, Mudgee, NSW, *bottom*: PWH (courtesy Mary Cadman); **44** MAAS; **45** PWH; **46** PWH; **48** BL (29920P); **49** *top*: CRM, *bottom*: PWH; **50** J. P. Campbell, Australia working 1900s, "Filling the boiler", from an untitled album, c.1900, gelatin silver photograph 7.9 x 13.0 cm, gift of Mrs A. C. Tyson 1983, Collection: Australian National Gallery, Canberra; **51** *top*: NLA, *bottom*: courtesy Florence Beaton (photo Clara McNabb); **52** Mus Childhood (P88.22); **53** *top*: NLA, *bottom*: PWH (attributed to Carl Praetz, Ballarat, Vic, 1890s); **54** *top*: Oxley (47551), *bottom*: MAAS; **55** MAAS; **57** courtesy *The News*, Adelaide; **58** *top*: PWH, *bottom*: MAAS; **59** *top*: Oxley (42716), *bottom*: PWH; **62** NLA (AIS photo); **63** *top*: PWH, *bottom*: MAAS; **64** KV Mus; **65** *top*: CRM (courtesy Mr D. Le Lievre); **66** BL (29805P); **68** AOIS; **70** PWH (attributed to Joan Fagg, Tumbarumba, NSW); **73** *top*: Oxley (5003), *bottom*: PWH; **74** Oxley (35238); **75** NLA; **76** NLA (Tilba Tilba Collection); **77** CRM; **78** Arch NSW (4/8566, Card 8205); **79** courtesy Mrs P Powell; **80** *top*: Oxley (42955), *bottom*: PWH; **82** NLA (AIS photo); **83** KV Mus; **85** NLA (Album "Old Sydney", 1877–94); **87** Mus Vic; **88** MAAS; **89** KV Mus; **92** Oxley (60506); **93** BL (29945P); **94** NLA; **97** BL (Mr Neil Mitchell Collection, 29429P); **100** *bottom*: MAAS; **101** *top*: Nicholas Caire, Australia 1837–1918, Bush hut, Gippsland, c.1884, gelatin silver printing out paper photo 15.0 x 20.2 cm, Collection: Australian National Gallery, Canberra, *bottom*: courtesy Mrs Meryl Plantinga; **104** *top*: ML (SSL:M B40700), *bottom*: Mus Vic; **106** BL (66492P); **107** Reg Morrison/Weldon Trannies; **108** *top*: RHS, Vic, *bottom*: BL (24597P); **110** ML (SSL:M B38362); **111** *top*: ML (SSL:M B38364, photo Mrs A. M. Hopewell), *bottom*: Laver Collection, by kind permission of Robert John Laver, Kadina, SA; **112** *top*: ML (SSL:M B44439), *bottom left*: BL (24341P), *bottom right*: BL (24340P); **113** *top*: BL (Royal Western Australian Historical Society Collection, 24229P), *bottom left*: BL (Mr Ian Crowe Collection, 28680P), *bottom right*: BL (Royal Western Australian Historical Society Collection, 24254P); **115** ML (SSL:M B48782); **116** BL (1440P); **117** PWH (courtesy Elsie Shepherd); **118** Mitchell; **119** BL (Royal Western Australian Historical Society Collection, 24400P); **121** NLA (AIS photo); **122** *top*: BL (67317P), *bottom*: BL (70868P); **124** BL (24922P); **128** *top*: ML (SSL:M B39315), *bottom*: BL (1850P); **130** *top*: BL (23985P), *bottom left*: Oxley (40720), *bottom right*: Oxley (36414); **131** *top*: Oxley (163922), *bottom*: NLA (Tilba Tilba Collection); **132** *top*: Oxley (44027), *bottom*: ML (SSL:M B48012); **133** *top*: BL (24000P), *bottom*: Oxley (142386); **136** ML (SSL:M B48797); **137** ML (SSL:M B20208); **138** Laver Collection, by kind permission of Robert John Laver, Kadina, SA; **139** Mus Childhood (P88.32); **140** *top*: BL (68114P), *bottom left*: Mus Childhood (P88.91), *bottom right*: Cons Comm (Chettle-Robb Collection); **141** NTA; **142** GL; **143** *top*: BL (26944P), *bottom*: Holbrook; **145** *top*: BL (5504P); **146** BL (28014P); **148** *top*: Laver Collection, by kind permission of Robert John Laver, Kadina, SA, *bottom*: BL (29914P); **150** NLA; **151** Mus Childhood (P87.126); **153** *top*: BL (68215P), *bottom left*: Oxley (14344), *bottom right*: BL (29875P); **156** *top*: Oxley (147559), *bottom left*: NLA (Tilba Tilba Collection), *bottom right*: BL (29927P); **157** *top*: Mus Childhood (P89.12), *bottom*: Cons Comm (Bradshaw Collection); **158** *top*: BL (29876P), *bottom*: Oxley (48665); **160** *top*: KV; **161** *bottom*: MAAS; **162** *top*: PWH, *bottom*: KV Mus; **163** PWH; **164** ANU/ABL, Australian Agricultural Company, 160/337; **165** *top*: Alice Springs Public Library, *bottom*: Laver Collection, by kind permission of Robert John Laver, Kadina, SA; **166–167** Laver Collection, by kind permission of Robert John Laver, Kadina, SA; **167** *bottom right*: NT Library; **168** Mus Childhood (P88.110); **169** *top*: BL (23758P), *bottom*: BL(66486P); **171** *top*: NLA (AIS photo), *bottom*: NLA (AIS photo); **172** *bottom*: PWH; **174–175** Arch Tas; **176** PWH; **178** *top*: NTA, *bottom*: NLA (photo: Ros Kampard); **180** Cons Comm (Bradshaw Collection); **183** courtesy Barbara James; **185** Cons Comm (Wuttke Collection); **186** Cons Comm (Bradshaw Collection); **187–188** Cons Comm (Bradshaw Collection); **190** courtesy Richmond River Historical Society; **192** NTSA; **194** Oxley (3680); **195** Oxley (63220); **196** Oxley (142351); **197** Oxley (64761); **198** Oxley (3681); **199** Oxley (172486); **201–205** courtesy Mona Byrne; **206** *top*: Cons Comm (Heaton Collection), *bottom*: NLA (Greenwood/Gillstrom Collection); **208** courtesy Barbara James; **210–211** courtesy Clive Hyde; **212** *top*: ML (SSL:M B30656); **215** *top*: Attributed to Helen Lambert, Australia working, c.1860–70, "My drawing room", Sydney, c.1869, from album *Who and what we saw at the Antipodes*, assembled 1868–70, albumen silver photograph, 13.5 x 19.1 cm, Collection: Australian National Gallery, Canberra, *bottom*: PWH; **218** BL (4554B/2); **219** *top*: BL (66181P), *bottom*: PWH (courtesy Wendy Hucker); **220–221** Uniting Church Frontier Services; **222** Oxley (38338); **223** Australian Archives, Vic (Aust Travel Industry Assoc CRS914); **224** *top*: RHS Vic; **226** Oxley (20215); **227** PWH; **229** *top*: NLA (Tilba Tilba Collection, *bottom*: BL (1893P); **230** *top*: BL (28306P), *bottom*: BL (28303P); **231** Cons Comm (Powell-Price Collection); **232** ML (SSL:M B30582); **233** PWH; **234** *top*: NTA, *bottom*: Cons Comm (Wuttke Collection); **235** ML (SSL:M B48530); **236** BL (66263P); **237** *top*: Arch Tas; **238** RHS Vic; **239** *top*: BL (3209P), *bottom*: courtesy Florence Beaton; **240** Arch Tas; **242** BL (23599P); **243** courtesy Mona Byrne; **244** BL (23615P).

# ABBREVIATIONS

AOIS: Australian Overseas Information Service;   Arch NSW: Archives Office of New South Wales;   Arch Tas: Archives Office of Tasmania;   BL: Battye Library, WA;   Cons Comm: Conservation Commission of the Northern Territory;   CRM: Cobar Regional Museum;   GL: Garnet Lord Collection, SA;   Holbrook: Holbrook Inn Museum, NSW;   KV: Kangaroo Valley Historical Society;   KV Mus: Kangaroo Valley Pioneer Farm Museum;   MAAS: Museum of Applied Arts & Sciences, Sydney;   Mitchell: Mitchell Library, State Library of New South Wales;   ML: Mortlock Library of South Australiana;   Mus Childhood: WACAE Museum of Childhood, Subiaco;   Mus Vic: Photo Archive Project, Museum of Victoria;   NLA: National Library of Australia;   NT Library: State Reference Library of the Northern Territory;   NTA: National Trust of Australia (Northern Territory);   NTSA: National Trust of South Australia;   OPHL: Old Parliament House Library, SA;   Oxley: John Oxley Library, Brisbane;   PWH: Pioneer Women's Hut, Tumbarumba, NSW;   RHS Vic: Royal Historical Society of Victoria.

# INDEX

*Page numbers in italics refer to illustrations.*